THE
STUDENT COMMUNITY
AT ABERDEEN
1860-1939

AUP titles of related interest

ABERDEEN AND THE ENLIGHTENMENT
edited by Jennifer J Carter and Joan H Pittock

WILLIAM ELPHINSTONE AND THE KINGDOM
OF SCOTLAND 1431–1514
Leslie J Macfarlane

EMIGRATION FROM NORTH-EAST SCOTLAND
Volume 1 Willing Exiles
Volume 2 Beyond the Broad Atlantic
Marjory Harper

NEW LIGHT ON MEDIEVAL ABERDEEN
edited by John S Smith

ABERDEEN IN THE NINETEENTH CENTURY
The Making of the Modern City
edited by John S Smith and David Stevenson

LITERATURE OF THE NORTH
edited by David Hewitt and Michael Spiller

THE GREIG-DUNCAN FOLK SONG COLLECTION
editors Patrick Shuldham-Shaw and Emily B Lyle

University of Aberdeen ROLL OF GRADUATES
1956–1970 with Supplement 1860–1955
compiled by Louise Donald and William S MacDonald

QUINCENTENNIAL STUDIES
in the history of
THE UNIVERSITY OF ABERDEEN

THE
STUDENT COMMUNITY
AT ABERDEEN
1860–1939

R D Anderson

Published for the University of Aberdeen by
ABERDEEN UNIVERSITY PRESS

First published 1988
Aberdeen University Press
A member of the Pergamon Group

© University of Aberdeen 1988

British Library Cataloguing in Publication Data

Anderson, R.D. (Robert David), *1942–*
    The student community at Aberdeen, 1860–1939.
    1. Scotland. Grampian Region. Aberdeen.
    Universities. University of Aberdeen.
    Students, 1860–1939
    I. Title   II. Series
    378′.198′0941235

    ISBN 0 08 036588 4

PRINTED IN GREAT BRITAIN
THE UNIVERSITY PRESS
ABERDEEN

Foreword

In 1995 the University of Aberdeen celebrates five hundred years of continuous existence. Some eighty other European universities had been established before 1500, of which about fifty have survived to the later twentieth century, though not all of those with an uninterrupted history. At Aberdeen, King's College and University was founded in 1495, and Marischal College in 1593, the two combining to form a single university in 1860. Such a long institutional life invites close historical study, as well as celebration; but the 1980s are not an easy time for British universities, and it is therefore the more striking that in 1984 the governing body of the University of Aberdeen decided to commission a series of historical studies in honour of the quincentenary. The decision to commit funds to this project, and to give the Editorial Board such a free hand as we have had, makes the University Court's decision the braver and more honourable.

After consulting colleagues here and elsewhere, including in particular historians familiar with the planning and progress of the multi-volume history of the University of Oxford, the Editorial Board at Aberdeen chose to launch a series of short scholarly studies, each coherent in itself, but together designed to illuminate and reinterpret Aberdeen University's history. While naturally wishing to emphasise what is particular to Aberdeen, we have sought to avoid parochialism by placing this university's affairs in as wide a context as possible, and also by involving scholars from outside Aberdeen in our work.

The first of the Quincentennial series to appear is by a scholar from Edinburgh University, well known for his writings on French and Scottish education in the nineteenth century. Hitherto university historians have tended to ignore the student community, or to treat it at best only anecdotally. In Dr R D Anderson's *The Student Community at Aberdeen 1860–1939* we have a thorough and perceptive examination of the composition of the student body at Aberdeen and of the traditions and experiences that influenced it. He links the academic with the informal activities of students over a long enough time-span to register considerable change; and he evaluates the extent and also the limitations of the corporate side of student life, focusing, for example, on organised sport, debating, music-making, and politics. Scottish universities were early to give official recognition to undergraduate opinion through students' representative institutions and Dr Anderson looks at the history of student representation at Aberdeen, including the revival in the nineteenth century of the ancient office of Rector. He shows how the official student viewpoint came to influence internal university affairs (not least the curriculum) as well as influencing external relations, especially those of the university with government and parliament. The extent of state intervention in British universities was much greater in the nineteenth century than is often appreciated, a point which this study reinforces. Dr Anderson pictures the experience of a particular, relatively advantaged group within British society in the forty years each side of 1900—a key period for Aberdeen which included (for example) the admission of women students to the university, and the trauma of the First World War, in which half of the young men in the University's Territorial Army Company were to be killed within a year of the beginning of hostilities. This systematic study of the student community at Aberdeen certainly adds to historical knowledge, and has a particular value in suggesting many wider considerations about the connections between universities and the societies they serve.

The Quincentennial Studies could not exist without the generosity and vision of the University Court, and the effort of many colleagues. Especial thanks are due to our governing committee, including its outside assessors Professor Donald Watt of St Andrews and Dr Robert Anderson of Edinburgh; to Dr John Fletcher of Aston, and Dr Gerald Aylmer of Oxford; to the staff of the Aberdeen University Library; and to the members of the Editorial Board: Professor John D Hargreaves, Dr Nicholas Fisher, Dr Leslie J Macfarlane, Mr Colin A McLaren, Dr David Stevenson, and Mr Donald J Withrington—who is the Commissioning Editor for this volume in the series.

JENNIFER CARTER
General Editor

Contents

FOREWORD   v
LIST OF ILLUSTRATIONS   viii
PREFACE   ix

INTRODUCTION   1
CHAPTER 1   Tradition and change from 1860 to the 1880s   6
CHAPTER 2   The corporate ideal   32
CHAPTER 3   Consolidation and development down to 1914   56
CHAPTER 4   War, peace and politics, 1914–1939   83
CONCLUSION   116

NOTES   119
APPENDIX I Figures and tables   130
APPENDIX II Rectorial elections   142
BIBLIOGRAPHICAL NOTE   146
INDEX   148

List of Illustrations

1 'Editorial staff of *Alma Mater*, 1889–90'. 2
2 'Domestic economy of the Macleans and the Macleods'. 4
3 'An old photograph' of students in about 1870. 8
4 'Our reunion dinner', 1896. 21
5 The Rectorial contest of 1884 in a contemporary cartoon. 29
6 The mastheads used for *Alma Mater*'s gossip columns. 35
7 'Students' Rectorial fight', 1896, from a painting. 39
8 'The Shinty Club, 1910–11'. 41
9 'Aberdeen University Arts Football Club, 1872–73'. 43
10 Concert programme, 4 March 1898. 50, 51
11 'The New Poets, or Obliging the Editor', a cartoon of 1911. 57
12 'The Gateway, King's College', a photograph of 1916. 62
13 Picnic group, 12 June 1909. 66, 67
14 The cast of the Boat Club farce, 1911. 69
15 'Billiard Room, University Union'. 70
16 The Shooting Club Team, 1910–11. 74
17 'The Unionist defence after the battle', photograph of the Rectorial fight, 1902. 79
18 'Linkie', Eric Linklater, 1925. 90
19 A scene from *Antigone*, 1919. 95
20 Cover of the Gala Rag Magazine, April 1931. 97
21 The Dramatic Society, 1936. 106
22 'The Adventures of Bertie the Bajan', 1928. 109

All the illustrations are reproduced by kind permission of Aberdeen University Library.

Author's Preface

This study is part of the series commissioned by the University of Aberdeen to commemorate the five hundredth anniversary of its foundation, and my first acknowledgement must be to the university for the courage and vision which it has shown in undertaking this project at a time of difficulty for universities everywhere. It was a particular act of faith to entrust a commission of this kind to a historian with no previous connection with Aberdeen, and I hope that this trust has been vindicated.

The general editor of the project, Jennifer Carter, and my commissioning editor, Donald Withrington, have been unstinting in their encouragement, advice and hospitality. I owe an equal debt to the university archivist, Colin McLaren. His expert guidance has steered me towards many sources which I should not have discovered for myself, and he and his staff have made the university archives an exceptionally pleasant and efficient place to conduct historical research.

Two types of source were impossible to use fully within the constraints of time and space which applied to my work. One is the local press, that almost inexhaustible source for the nineteenth-century historian. I am most grateful to Caroline Gimingham for providing research assistance on this source. Her patient work, even when it was seemingly negative, underlies many of the conclusions in my text.

The other source is the memories of those who were students in the 1920s and 1930s. I was unable to carry out interviews myself, but I have been fortunate to see transcripts of some of the taped interviews and to read the written memoirs collected as part of the Quincentenary History Project. I have decided not to make direct citations from this evidence, but it has influenced much of what I say about those years, and I hope that those who lived through them will not find my account, based mainly on written sources, too unrecognisable.

I am also grateful to many friends and colleagues at Edinburgh University for information and advice. Any errors are, of course, my responsibility.

I received a personal research grant from the British Academy, and a similar grant from the Travel and Research Committee of Edinburgh University, to cover the cost of visiting Aberdeen, and I am happy to acknowledge this help.

Introduction

The modern University of Aberdeen was founded by the amalgamation or 'fusion' of King's College and Marischal College in 1860. It retained close links with the largely agricultural north-eastern region of Scotland which it served, and the shared background of its students gave them a natural sense of community and identity. Like students at all Scottish universities until recently, they lived at home or in lodgings, and the forms of student life which they developed were very different from the Oxford and Cambridge model. This history therefore deals, among other things, with the relation of the student community to the urban community around it. It will also argue that the late nineteenth century saw the growth of a 'corporate' ideal of student life, as something more intensive and enclosed, which deepened the influence of the university in shaping the values of the professional and business elite which it formed. Chapter 1 looks at the life of the university at a time when traditional habits still predominated. Chapter 2 concentrates on the innovations in student life between the 1870s and 1890s, and chapter 3 shows how they developed in the years before 1914. Chapter 4 covers the period between 1914 and 1939, special attention being paid to the questions of war, peace and politics which dominated that era.

There is no reason to think that developments at Aberdeen were fundamentally different from those in the other Scottish universities, or indeed in the non-residential university colleges which grew up in provincial England. The histories written about the latter suggest close parallels. The history of Scottish universities has been neglected, but what has been written says little about student life. It is therefore difficult to put the Aberdeen story in context, and it has been written as if it were self-contained, but the reader should remember that very similar things were happening elsewhere. Sometimes Aberdeen pioneered innovations, but more often perhaps, especially in intellectual and political matters, it lagged behind Edinburgh and Glasgow, larger universities which enjoyed the stimulus of a more complex urban environment.

1

1 'Editorial staff of *Alma Mater*, 1889–90'. Back row (left to right) K Gill-ies, W Bulloch, T W Ogilvie, J M Bulloch, W P Grant, G Duncan, D Mac-millan; centre (sitting) A Mitchell, A Mackay; front row, J H Barron, R B Robson, J D Symon. Frontispiece of *AM*, 7 (24 April 1889).

The historian approaching this subject has no shortage of material—above all, the records of student organisations and the student press. Aberdeen had one of the earliest student magazines with a continuous history, *Alma Mater*, founded in 1883, and supplemented by the newspaper *Gaudie* from 1934. These journals are unrivalled as a source of information about events and opinions, but the fullness of coverage depended on the zeal of volunteer reporters or club secretaries, and the editorial direction was often in the hands of a clique who might not be representative of university life as a whole. In each period, student editors tended to follow the journalistic fashions of their day, and since *Alma Mater* was a magazine rather than a newspaper this often meant concentration on fiction, verse or humour rather than hard news.

The problem of how representative student activists are is a more general one. The historian's conception of 'student life' inevitably concentrates on politics, debating, clubs and societies, sport, and the more visible forms of social life such as dining, drinking and dancing. But in a university like Aberdeen, with many poorer students from country backgrounds, those who engaged in these activities were probably a minority. For many, studying was the main part of student life. The deepest effects of a university education are the intellectual influences which mould a student's beliefs, and the emotional and spiritual experiences which accompany the achievement of adult status. The former involves the history of the curriculum, and largely falls outside the scope of this study, while the more intimate aspects of student life are difficult to say much about in the absence of diaries, private letters and similar sources. It is with the public life of the student community, therefore, that we shall be largely concerned.

Another difficulty, perhaps peculiar to Aberdeen, is the accretion of myth around the subject of student life. Its more picturesque aspects attracted nineteenth-century writers, and a literary genre grew up which stressed the contrast of red gown and grey granite, the humble social origins of the students, the austere and competitive intellectual ethos symbolised by the system of entrance bursaries, and the struggle with poverty in lonely lodgings. Articles on these themes appeared regularly in Victorian magazines, culminating in 1874 in the novel *Life at a Northern University* by Neil N Maclean, who had been a student at King's College in the 1850s.[1] This was generally accepted as a realistic account, and went into several editions. Its characters include an impoverished Highland student who dies of overwork after achieving a brilliant academic success, and this was an especially popular theme which became part of the literary myth of the 'lad of parts'. One of those who helped to create this myth, by promoting the 'kailyard' school of literature, was the journalist and writer William Robertson Nicoll, an Aberdeen graduate of the 1860s.[2]

Fictional accounts of Aberdeen student life include the dialect novels of George MacDonald in the 1860s, which contemporary student readers did not find convincing, and stories by Gordon Stables, a student at Marischal College just before 1860, who became a naval surgeon and a highly successful writer of adventure stories for boys: the title of his *From Ploughshare to Pulpit: a Tale of the Battle of Life* (1895), which was cast in the mould of *Life at a Northern University*, sums up the Aberdeen literary image. This was also expressed through poetry, and sentimentalists liked to quote Walter C Smith's evocation of life:

> In the old University town,
> Looking out on the cold North Sea,
> 'Twixt the Minster towers and the College crown.[3]

The 'crown' was the crown spire of King's College Chapel, and King's College, set in the ancient community of Old Aberdeen, attracted far more sentimental feeling than Marischal. Emotional recollection of the physical setting of student life was a hallmark of the writing of William Keith Leask, whose name will recur frequently, along with that of J M Bul-

2   'Domestic economy of the Macleans and the Macleods', G Stables, *From Ploughshare to Pulpit: a Tale of the Battle of Life* (London, 1895), facing p. 233.

loch. Bulloch was a student activist of the 1880s who spent his professional life as a London journalist, but never cut his ties with the university; Leask was an older man who returned to Aberdeen as an assistant in the 1880s, and, having failed to secure the Chair of Greek on which he had set his heart, thereafter lived a rather embittered and impoverished life as an independent scholar.[4] Leask and Bulloch contributed frequently to *Alma Mater* in its early days, and kept up the connection until their deaths in 1925 and 1938 respectively, tending the cult of the university and of the ideal of student life shaped by Bulloch's generation. Leask collected many of his pieces, which are often unreliable for dates and facts, in a book called *Interamna Borealis* (1917).

Leask and Bulloch also helped to set the tone of the *Aberdeen University Review*, a magazine for alumni founded in 1913. It was the first such magazine in Scotland, and alumnus feeling for Aberdeen was always especially strong. An Aberdeen University Club, founded in London in 1884 to hold regular dinners, was the prototype of many all over the world. More specific to Aberdeen was a unique source, the 'arts class records'. Until the 1890s all arts students went through the same curriculum, and had a strong *esprit de corps*. They usually appointed a secretary, whose task it became to keep in touch with members, arrange reunions, and publish periodic records. Sometimes these were simply an account of the reunion dinner or an updating of news about members, but some were elaborate works which included systematic recollections of student days and very full biographical data, which are an important source for the social historian. For classes later than 1900 there are few such records, but their role was taken over by the *Review*, which also published valuable recollections. However, those who choose to recall their student days in print are inevitably those who remember them with affection and value a continuing link with the university; the experience of unhappy, disaffected or non-gregarious students goes unrecorded. All sources have their biases and their lacunae, and in student life as elsewhere those whose activities leave written traces enjoy more than their fair share of the historian's attention.

Chapter 1

Tradition and Change from 1860 to the 1880s

The united University of Aberdeen came into existence in 1860 following the Universities (Scotland) Act of 1858, which gave a more or less uniform constitution and curriculum to all the Scottish universities. More closely tied to the national system than before, the university continued to draw most of its students from the surrounding region. Their numbers began to rise steadily in the 1870s, and reached a peak in 1890, after which there was a decline. The heart of the university remained the arts faculty, which trained ministers and teachers, but its position was soon challenged by the new medical school. Though the latter saw considerable fluctuations of prosperity, its students far outnumbered those in the other professional faculties, law and divinity.[1]

After 1860, arts and divinity were based at King's College in Old Aberdeen, law and medicine at Marischal College a mile away, and the two colleges remained distinct communities in very different physical settings. Old Aberdeen retained its calm and semi-ecclesiastical atmosphere, while Marischal College was in the heart of the city, its facade obscured until the end of the century by dingy shops and tenements, but only a stone's throw from Union Street, the main centre of fashion and social activity. It was also near the Royal Infirmary and other hospitals, attendance at which took up much of a medical student's time. The fundamental division in the student community was thus between arts men at King's and medicals at Marischal. In the 1860s and 1870s the life of King's is better documented, partly because of the class records, partly because the survival of pre-1860 traditions attracted more attention. But the medicals, who tended to be older and better off than the arts students, were to pioneer new forms of student activity.

Before approaching that subject, we may attempt a collective portrait of the student body, based on precise information rather than literary impressions. Where did they come from, how old were they, what were their social origins, and what careers were they aiming at? Three arts class records, those of 1864, 1866 and 1868, providing a total sample of 343 students, have been analysed in order to answer these questions, and the results can be studied in detail in the tables in Appendix I.

The birthplaces of students (see Table 4) show that three-quarters came from the North East—17.5 per cent from Aberdeen itself, and the rest from the surrounding counties. The remaining quarter divided about equally between students from the Highlands, the rest of Scotland, and England and overseas; in the medical faculty the last group would undoubtedly have been larger, for Aberdeen's reputation attracted many English and colonial students.

While the geographical origins of students were to change little in future years, this cannot be said of the age at which they arrived (Table 5). By modern standards, the age-range was remarkably wide, but in the 1860s the majority came up between the ages of 15 and 17. A few came at 14 or even 13, but this was (contrary perhaps to legend) an essentially middle-class habit, being particularly common for sons of the manse. One of these who entered the 1866 class at 13, Robert Neil, proved to be its academic star, eventually becoming a Cambridge don. The thirteen-year-olds did include (in 1868) George Sorrie, the son of a labourer from Kintore, one of the few indisputably poor students in the sample. But working-class students were more likely to be found among the significant number who came, as in all the Scottish universities at this time, in their twenties. Traditionally, they were men who had felt a call to the ministry in adult life, but a new group who can be identified in the 1860s were those who had stayed on at school under the 'pupil-teacher' system and had qualified as teachers and taught for a time before mobilising their resources to come to the university for a degree. Teacher training, subsidised by the state, had become an important channel of social mobility and was later to be brought within the university sphere.

The age pattern and the comparative youth of most arts students reflected the Scottish school system. Even town secondary schools which were well equipped to give a classical and mathematical training did not keep their pupils beyond 15. After this, a middle-class boy could go directly into business or, if he was destined for a learned profession, to the university. There was no school-leaving examination, and no test for university entry. In practice, some knowledge of Latin was essential, but the first-year ('junior') university classes in Latin, Greek, and mathematics began at a very elementary level, which made things easier for adult students and pupils from rural parish schools. The direct link between parish school and university was a prized feature of the Scottish educational tradition, and was at its strongest in the North East, being reinforced by the Dick Bequest, a local trust which gave substantial financial encouragement to teachers with high university qualifications. Such men would coach their best pupils in Latin and prepare them for bursaries, and there

3 'An old photograph' of W L Mollison, Robert Smith, W M Ramsay and
R A Neil, about 1870. The book among the beer bottles is Rossetti's *Poems*.
The photograph was reproduced in *AM*, 27 (8 December 1909), p. 73.

were many rural schools famous for their university successes. University
preparation in parish schools also remained common in the Highlands,
because there were so few towns with secondary schools.

The Aberdeen bursary competition was a famous institution which
remained in full vigour. Most of the bursaries endowed over the years

were awarded through a single open examination. This was later shifted to Easter, but traditionally it was in October that candidates arrived in Aberdeen from all parts to wrestle with papers in which Latin composition held the place of honour. The marks and order of merit were published in full, and local interest was intense. The competition supplied a common target for teachers, and its prestige was such that most local students attempted it, including those from middle-class families; there was no stigma of poverty attached to being a bursar. This meant, of course, that the funds were no longer giving specific help to poorer students. Moreover, the secondary schools in the city specialised in the bursary examination and usually won the best places, so that it became common even for boys educated in country schools to spend a year or so in Aberdeen to receive their final polish. In the 1860s the three schools involved were Aberdeen Grammar School, Old Aberdeen Grammar School ('the Barn') and the Gymnasium or 'Gym', otherwise Chanonry House School, which was a socially select private school, including boarders. The 'Gym' and the 'Barn' were effectively part of the King's 'campus', and their pupils would already be familiar with university life. Others too would usually know exactly what to expect, and how to behave, from fathers, brothers, schoolmasters, or ministers who were Aberdeen alumni. The Gymnasium closed down in 1887, and the 'Barn' in 1892, being too small to compete with modern secondary schools, but their place was taken by Robert Gordon's College, formed in 1881 by turning a traditional residential 'hospital' into a large day school.

The arts class records include details of schooling. Many students attended several schools, which makes an exact breakdown difficult, but approximate figures can be given. Twenty-seven per cent had been educated entirely in Aberdeen; these were mainly, of course, the city-born students, and better-off families often used small private 'academies' before sending their sons to one of the big three. The largest group, 37 per cent, had been educated at a parish or similar local school before finishing off at Aberdeen, while only 17 per cent came direct from a parish school. A further 13 per cent came from Scottish urban schools like Elgin, Banff or Inverness Academies. The rest were educated privately or outside Scotland, though none of the sample had been to an English public school. Counting a few who began their schooling outside Scotland and finished it in Aberdeen, two-thirds of the students had been to one of the Aberdeen secondary schools. This close relationship of the university with the local and regional school system which it drew on for the bulk of its students, and supplied with succeeding generations of teachers, was perhaps unique to Aberdeen.

From the 1870s, however, secondary education experienced important changes, notably a rise in the leaving age and the development of urban schools with a strong academic bias. University preparation in parish schools became difficult, and rural secondary work became concentrated in selected schools. As part of this policy, the Scotch Education Department (as it was then called) introduced the school Leaving Certificate in 1888, which was normally taken at 17, and when the universities introduced an entrance examination in 1892 this was fixed at the same level. After that it was difficult to get to the university without an extended secondary schooling. But as Table 5 shows, the rise in the age of entry was a steady movement already under way in the 1860s. In 1860 the commonest age of entry was 15; by 1900 it was 18, and only a handful of students were under 17. This upward shift in the age pattern, and the greater maturity which it implied, clearly had considerable implications for students' social life and attitudes.

Table 7 shows the occupations of the arts students' fathers. Although in many cases these were not recorded, and the relation between occupation and social status may be ambiguous, the data are in line with all that we know about the Scottish universities: the majority came from professional, business or farming families, with a significant minority from lower down the social scale. At Aberdeen, farmers were the largest single group of parents, followed by ministers. Farming, of course, covers a wide social range: at one end were parents described as 'gentleman farmer' or 'distinguished agriculturist'; at the other, there may have been a number of small farmers, though only one was described as a crofter. The largest 'democratic' element came from the groups defined as 'intermediate' and 'working-class' in Table 7: small shopkeepers and artisans in Aberdeen itself or the small towns of the region. Joiners, shoemakers, blacksmiths and similar members of the traditional skilled trades could aspire to having a son at the university. But few parents belonged to the unskilled or rural working class—one labourer, one farm servant, a handful of gamekeepers and gardeners—and none at all came from modern industry, except perhaps for a woolspinner at Tillicoultry. Neither the fishing industry of the North East nor the factories of Aberdeen sent a single student. We therefore have to be cautious in accepting the traditional accounts of student poverty. Many Aberdeen students came from prosperous middle-class families— their fathers were merchants, manufacturers, bankers, doctors, lawyers, government officials and the like. Many others, perhaps a majority, were the sons of country ministers and schoolmasters, or small businessmen and modest farmers, for whom university attendance might well involve family sacrifices and a way of life constrained by constant economies; but those from really poor backgrounds were a small minority, albeit one whose very presence was notable. So too, the impression given in *Life at a Northern University* of a colony of impoverished Highland students living in garrets does not seem valid for the 1860s. Of the 26 from the Highlands and Islands in the sample of 343, most were the sons of farmers and ministers, solicitors and farm managers; only one, the son of an Inverness cabinetmaker and upholsterer, can be classified (rather doubtfully) as 'working class'. Besides, as Table 4 shows, Highland students were significantly less numerous than they became later, though they did play a distinctive part in student social life.

Most Aberdeen students had a career clearly in mind, and since the class records have details of their later careers, it is possible to relate the origins of students to their 'destinations', and to see what social transformation a university education wrought. This is shown in Table 8. The chief outlets were the church, medicine and teaching, but the table also shows the significance of overseas careers. Aberdeen had a well-known connection with the Indian Civil Service (and similar careers like the Chinese Consular Service), and other students went abroad as farmers in America or Australia, or planters in Ceylon and British Guiana. Many of the doctors, ministers, teachers and businessmen also spent their working lives abroad, and this was the experience of about a quarter of Aberdeen graduates. By a very broad calculation, the North East of Scotland, the rest of Scotland, and England and Wales each accounted for a further quarter, the diaspora of Aberdeen-trained doctors being particularly conspicuous.[2]

Thus the university made the North East an exporter of talent—a factor which surely helps to explain why nostalgia for the *alma mater* was so strong. For individuals, it was also a channel of social mobility, and Table 8 illustrates some of the subtleties of social status. Those who were upwardly mobile favoured the church and teaching, but neither made much appeal to the professional classes, apart from ministers' sons following their fathers. Doctors' sons were the most likely to choose their father's profession, though they had no monopoly of medicine, which drew on a wide social range. There was also a good deal of lateral mobility between the professions and business, and it has been claimed that 'Aberdeen University . . . acted as a channel diverting the children of business families away from business and into professions'.[3] But this was not necessarily so, for families were likely to send a son to university only if they already had a professional career in mind. Thus none of the numerous farmers' sons at Aberdeen went into farming (except, in a few cases, abroad), which probably means that these were younger sons being diverted into alternative careers while a brother inherited the farm. In the same way, businessmen had no strong motive for giving a university education to sons who were to inherit their business. Contemporary wisdom held, in any case, that the best training for business was experience, and that entry to it should not be delayed too long. Therefore university students were not a representative cross-section of middle-class youth, and in this light the number who took up business careers, mostly in commerce rather than industry, seems quite high given Aberdeen's rural hinterland and the traditionalism of the Scottish curriculum.

The class records show that those who took up business often followed a distinctive pattern of attendance for one or two years of the curriculum without taking a degree. Some parents evidently used the arts classes as a form of liberal education before their sons went into the family firm, a practice which died out as secondary schools improved; others made use of the university mathematics and science classes as part of a business training. Two students who entered the 1864 class at the age of 14 illustrate a common pattern: Walter Cowan, son of the chief engineer of the Great North of Scotland Railway, stayed for two years before going to train as an engineer in France and Germany, eventually becoming an iron merchant; Lewis Pirie, son of a divinity professor (later principal of the university) studied mathematics and science for two years, then became an engineer in Glasgow and ran businesses in Liverpool and South Africa.

This was possible because of the flexibility of the system. Each year was self-contained, and so-called 'private students' could take a single class in one subject. Studies could be interrupted and resumed later, at Aberdeen or elsewhere, and by no means all students took the full four-year course. Of the 126 members of the class of 1868, 28 were private students. Others left at the end of each year, and only 69 per cent completed four years. But that was considered exceptionally high, and the figures for 1864 (59 per cent) and 1866 (56 per cent) were more typical.[4] In the early 1870s, annual averages show 108 students in the first-year classes, 62 completing the arts curriculum, and only 44 actually graduating.[5] The largest group of early leavers were medical students following the usual custom of taking some arts classes first; many indeed took the full course, and about a third of the medical graduates in the 1860s already had the MA.[6] For divinity four years of arts were compulsory, and those aiming at teaching were also likely to complete the course. But even these students did not necessarily take the MA examinations and graduate. The churches demanded only evidence of attendance, while for other careers like the Indian Civil Service it was the entrance examination, not a formal university qualification, which was decisive. At this stage of university history, degrees were relatively unimportant and their possession brought few special advantages.

Thus the arts classes were less homogeneous than the emphasis of the class records on common experience and *esprit de corps* might imply. They contained men of very different ages, who were using what the university offered as part of their own educational and career plans. Socially, the university was performing a number of functions. The most basic was to keep up the local supply of doctors, lawyers, ministers and teachers; but while this elite was replenished from below from the sons of farmers, shopkeepers or artisans, the university also gave local men the chance to compete in a wider British and imperial arena. And although Aberdeen students may be broadly defined as middle-class, many of them came from a background where the class divisions of modern industrial society had not fully developed, being brought up in villages and small towns, and educated at local schools used by a wide spread of classes. If such men were to compete for posts with their English contemporaries, to have successful professional careers in London and the English provinces, or to uphold the British way of life abroad as officials or businessmen, the university would need to give these sons of farmers and country ministers a social training which would allow them to blend into patterns increasingly dictated by the English public school ideal. The development of new forms of student life owed much to this demand.

If not all students completed the MA course, nearly all started the first year together as 'bajans'. One tradition which survived unselfconsciously was the designation of the four successive years—bajans, semis, tertians and magistrands. Another, which it soon became necessary to try to enforce or revive, was the wearing of the red gown or *toga rubra* by arts students. This was required by university regulations, but enforcement was left to student opinion. In 1870 student pressure brought the intro-duction of the 'trencher' or mortar-board.[7] Affording little warmth and vulnerable to wind, it was, like the short, sleeveless gown, singularly unsuited to the Aberdeen climate. The trencher was an innovation, and illustrated a new desire to elaborate distinctive and dignified traditions. But by the 1880s gown-wearing was in decline, and campaigns to enforce it, which continued at regular intervals until the 1930s, were never entirely successful. At some periods the red gown almost died out, at others it became quite popular, but it never again became universal, nor was it extended outside the arts faculty. When worn, it was considered correct for the gown to be old and ragged, and a naive bajan who wore one in pristine condition soon found himself set on by his seniors. 'Gown-tearing' was part of a more general ritual of ragging or 'crushes', in which the first-year students at King's were pushed and manhandled on the stairs and at the classroom doors.

The bajan class *par excellence* was Greek. Three subjects were normally studied each year, and in the first year these were junior Latin, junior

Greek and English. In the second year, classics continued with senior Latin and senior Greek, and junior mathematics began the study of science, which continued in the third year with senior mathematics and junior natural philosophy. The third year introduced mental philosophy in the shape of logic, and in the fourth year this continued with moral philosophy. The fourth year also included a compulsory class in natural history (the only class for which arts students had to visit Marischal), an optional one in senior natural philosophy, and a weekly lecture on Christian evidences, given by one of the divinity professors. Thus students covered three literary subjects in five annual courses, three scientific ones in four or five courses, and two philosophy courses: philosophy was hardly as central to the Scottish curriculum as is often claimed, and the importance of science as well as classics should be stressed. The third year was especially hard going for those without a mathematical flair, and many had recourse, especially if they were aiming at civil service or similar examinations, to private coaches, of whom the most famous was 'Davie' Rennet, who was active from 1860 into the twentieth century.[8]

Lectures were given five days a week, and since some subjects were taught for two separate hours, there were normally four hours of lecturing, from 9 a.m. to 1.15 p.m., with a break between 11 and 11.15 a.m. Students then returned to their homes or lodgings for dinner, and were free to read or to work on the written exercises set by most professors. There was no evening activity at King's, and thus little need for social facilities there. During the morning break, there was time to visit a baker's shop in the High Street of Old Aberdeen for apple tarts or 'hot and savoury fruitcakes'—though later jam scones became established as the traditional snack.[9] By the 1880s there was a sparsely furnished 'cloakroom', where students could shelter from the weather, congregate before and after classes, and hold such meetings as might be called for.

The timetable was thus well filled and the pace of work intensive. But the session was short, running from the end of October to the end of March, with about a week's break at Christmas. Lectures took up twenty weeks, followed by a fortnight of examinations in March, each subject being examined at the end of the year when it was taken. Under the post-1858 system it was also possible to take the MA with honours, and one in four or five students did this. But there were no special honours classes; honours students did extra reading and were examined in one of four specialised fields, but still had to take the ordinary curriculum in full, and were expected, like others, to complete their degree within four years.

The arts session ended with a graduation ceremony around 1 April. Students (and their professors) thus had a six-month summer vacation, a custom originally intended to allow students to take part in the summer farm work, or earn an income to support them through the winter. A

French official visitor in the 1860s had read about Scottish students working in the fields, but on inquiry he was told by the principal that 'there may have been one or two examples of this kind, but in general the students of this university . . . were the sons of fairly prosperous farmers'; if they worked, it was to pass the time or to help their parents, not out of necessity.[10] Though direct evidence about vacation habits is sparse, some students certainly took advantage of the expansion of upper-class tourism to work as ghillies, beaters, golf-caddies or sailors on pleasure steamers.[11] Most probably stayed with their families, joining in their visits to the seaside or the Highlands. The more adventurous or prosperous could travel on the continent, and there are accounts of visits to the standard tourist circuit—the Rhine, Switzerland, Italy. Men with scientific or academic ambitions might spend a few months in a German medical or university centre, and there were some classical enthusiasts who reached Greece, proudly scratching their names and that of their university on the marble at ancient sites.[12]

For medical students the summer was less leisurely, since there was a twelve-week summer session between May and July, which could not be avoided if the curriculum was to be got through and the three 'professional examinations' passed in the standard four years. The medical curriculum was complex, because as well as professorial lectures it included clinical sessions and practical classes at the Royal Infirmary and other institutions like the Sick Children's Hospital, the Royal Lunatic Asylum, and the Dispensary, which provided out-patient and maternity services to the poor. The conditions of admission to these independently run hospitals, and the fees charged, were frequent subjects for complaint. Like arts students, medical students went through the same classes together and developed a strong sense of comradeship, intensified by initiation into a professional ethos and by daily contact with poverty and suffering. They were generally older than arts students: if Scottish, they had commonly attended arts courses first, while the English and overseas students attracted to Aberdeen were likely to have had a more prolonged schooling. Since attendance at other medical schools could be counted for the Aberdeen degree, and since the so-called 'chronics' could stay on indefinitely resitting failed examinations, medical students generally had more diverse backgrounds and patterns of study.

Divinity and law students were few in number and played little part in wider university life. The usual divinity course took three years following the MA, but the four Aberdeen professors belonged to the Established Church, and many graduates went instead to the independent Free Church College in Aberdeen, or to Edinburgh or Glasgow. In law there was only one teaching post, and lectures were given in alternate years on Scots law and conveyancing. These were the minimum university requirements for the legal profession, and the classes were attended almost exclusively by men working in legal offices in the city, not full-time students. There was no Aberdeen law degree, and those with higher ambitions had to go to Edinburgh.

However 'student life' outside the classroom might develop, attending lectures and studying took up a large part of a student's time, and were at the centre of the university experience. When there was a common curriculum, and when the professors gave all the lectures in their subject—a minimum of a hundred—their personalities inevitably made a powerful impression, as all recollections of this period show. Lectures were compulsory, and attendance was checked by roll-calls or by handing in matriculation cards; in arts, there were fixed places allocated alphabetically, no doubt to help the professors remember names. Lecturing in the strict sense did not take up all the time: in classics in particular, the atmosphere was more school-like, with the professor going through texts and calling on individual students, and in other subjects a second daily hour was often devoted to oral interrogations or practical exercises. In the larger classes (Latin, Greek, mathematics, natural philosophy) there were assistants who helped with this practical work and with marking, but these were temporary posts for young men, and a true non-professorial staff did not yet exist.

Lectures were a communal experience with an interactive social tradition of their own. It was customary for professors to start each lecture with a short prayer, to give occasional disciplinary reprimands or moral advice, and to bring out venerable jokes for student approval. Student feelings were made clear by foot-stamping or 'ruffing' for approval, and foot-scraping for disapproval. There was also a tradition of lively behaviour before the professor arrived, which took the everyday form of communal singing, and the more boisterous one of 'passing up' students over the heads of their fellows from the front of the tiered lecture theatre to the back. At Christmas, popular professors got turkeys, cakes, bottles of whisky and other gifts from their class. Unpopular ones could receive rough treatment: in 1862, for example, after a disciplinary decision which was considered unjust, the professor of Latin was followed to his home by a jeering procession and pelted with stones.[13] The disciplinary powers of the Senatus were quite often called on, though everyday order was maintained effectively by the sacrists at King's and Marischal, usually imposing but kindly ex-soldiers who had a large place in student affections.

Students who came from Aberdeen lived with their families, and the rest either with relatives or family friends or in lodgings. No aspect of student life attracted more literary romance than the scantily-furnished garrets in which poor students fed themselves from a store of oatmeal and dried herrings. According to Neil Maclean, writing in 1872:

> A bag of meal, in which some eggs have been carefully packed, and another of potatoes, with a small kit of salt herrings, form their staple articles of food, on which they will be contented to live during the whole winter, provided they can drink in the words of knowledge that fall from their professors' lips.

Robertson Nicoll, who came to Aberdeen in 1866, claimed to 'know of at least one case where a student was practically starved to death with a huge empty oatmeal barrel beside him in his little garret',[14] while Bulloch, a student of the 1880s, though conceding that 'even in my days the hardy porridge brigade of country Bajans had disappeared', liked to recall a student who lived for a year in a herring-boat laid up in the harbour.[15]

Most students had more prosaic lodgings in a 'parlour-bedroom'. Country students might still bring a supply of oatmeal, butter or eggs, and there were those who bought their own food for the landlady to cook, like a student of the 1900s whose daily fare was a penny haddock.[16] But it was more usual for the landlady to provide meals—breakfast, dinner, and tea or supper in the early evening—and for the traditional ingredients to come in the form of her porridge and kippers rather than out of barrels. Most lodgings were in New Aberdeen, which meant that King's students had to walk some distance to classes. The walking route was via the Spital, where students had to run the gauntlet of the local urchins, who had a special chant—'Buttery Willie Collie'—directed against those brave enough to wear red gowns. A primitive bus was replaced in the 1870s by a tramway along King Street, and the development of this area offered new opportunities for lodgings, as did the Kittybrewster-Bedford Road area, which was convenient for King's. But by the end of the century the classic location for student digs, within easy reach of Marischal and Union Street, was Rosemount. All these were 'respectable' tenement areas, without garrets but with flats large enough for one or two rooms to be rented out. Landladies were commonly widows or spinsters for whom letting was a business, and generations of students grew familiar with their battered furniture, stained carpets, and pious or sentimental pictures. It does not seem to have been common either to take rooms with middle-class families, or to live in the poorer areas of the town. In later years, with the improvement of railway services and the introduction of the bicycle, it became more common for students living near Aberdeen to commute rather than take lodgings.

Literary accounts perhaps exaggerate the cheapness of living. Robertson Nicoll claimed to have paid only 2s. 6d. per week for accommodation, and 4s. 0d. for food. More realistic recollections suggest that shared rooms could be obtained for 3s. 6d. or 4s. 0d., but to this would have to be added 1s. 0d. for coals and gas in the winter, and about 10s. 0d. for meals. The *Lancet*, in a survey of medical schools in 1894, found Aberdeen the cheapest place in Britain, and thought it possible to live comfortably for 12s. 0d. But *Alma Mater* was sceptical about this, and the evidence suggests that by then reasonable lodgings with board would cost 15s. 0d. a week, good ones £1; in 1913 a range between 12s. 0d. and 23s. 6d. was mentioned.[17] Thus for the six-month session a student could survive on £20, though this would not cover books, clothes, extra meals, or entertainment. There were also the university fees to be paid. Each class was charged at two or three guineas, and fees had to be paid in full at the beginning of the year. In arts the annual fees, including a matriculation fee of £1, came to £8. 7s. 0d. in the first two years; £9. 8s. 0d. in the third; £7. 6s. 0d. in the fourth. Examination and graduation fees added three guineas to the cost of an arts degree. In medicine, the double session, hospital fees, and high examination fees (twenty guineas to cover the full course) made the costs considerably higher.[18]

For an arts student not living at home, fees and lodgings could not be cut to much less than £30 a year. Some income could be earned by private teaching or coaching, but bursaries were the commonest extra resource. Bursaries were still being founded by benefactors, and by the 1880s there were some 230 attached to the arts faculty, which meant that about half the students were bursars. Each year about forty bursaries became available, but their value depended on a student's place in the competition, not his financial need. About ten a year were worth from £30 to £40, which would certainly cover fees (which bursars still had to pay) and most living expenses. Half a dozen others were over £20, but the majority were between £10 and £20, and would need to be supplemented from family resources. Thus bursaries had their limitations, especially as they were paid in arrears in two 'moieties', at the beginning of February (advanced to January in 1888) and the end of the session; and while bursaries were numerous in arts and divinity, only a handful existed for medicine. Even so, this was a very significant system of support, and put university education within reach of families who could not otherwise have thought of it.

In an article on 'student life in Scotland' in 1860, the *Cornhill Magazine* concluded that the chief defect of the Scottish universities was the absence of 'corporate feeling'. There was plenty of studying, but in current usage:

> the name of student life is not given to the solitary turning of pages and wasting of midnight oil—to the mastering of Greek particles and the working of the differential calculus, but to the amusements of young men when they have thrown aside their books, to the alliances which they form, to the conversations they start, to their hunting, to their boating, to their fencing, to their drinking, to their love-making,—in a word, to their social ways.[19]

All these activities, apart from hunting, were eventually to be cultivated. But recollections of the 1860s and 1870s agree that organised social life was sparse. Until the development of athletics, Saturday was a day for walking or visiting friends. Sundays were confined by the strict sabbatarianism of the age. There was a morning service at King's College Chapel, which students of the Established Church were officially supposed to attend; the custom was well observed at first, but by the 1880s was declining. It meant a special journey out to King's, and it was easier to sample the preaching in city churches, one form of entertainment of which Aberdeen was not short. For secular amusements, students also fell back on local resources. In the words of the *Cornhill* the social life of Scottish students 'more strongly resembles the town life of young men than what is understood by student life'.[20] Their habits of sociability were still those familiar to readers of Dickens and Thackeray, centred on the steaming punchbowl and on songs and speechifying. The most basic form of amusement was an evening at a friend's lodgings, with convivial discussion around a bowl of toddy, some bottles of beer, or more solid refreshment. 'It was common then', according to Leask, 'for a friend to visit another with a carpet bag full of tarts, cakes, oranges, locust-beans, and a cocoanut'.[21]

The shadow of the landlady, however, made an evening in a pub more relaxing. Near King's there was the Red Lion, but the favourite hostelries were in the town centre: the City, the Lemon Tree and Duffus's, establishments with private rooms where an evening could be enlivened with card-playing and singing. For the more dissipated there were billiard-rooms, and a Friday or Saturday evening might end in a noisy return home, putting out street lights, stealing door knockers or shop signs, scrapping with young townsmen, and occasionally falling foul of the police, who were expected to be tolerant of these student pranks. One occasion on which they were traditional was 'bursary night' in February, when the bajans were expected to emerge from their shells, and bursars, flush with money, would 'visit the shrines of Venus or Bacchus'. The 'shrines of Venus' were probably not brothels, but the local girls' schools, which it was the custom to besiege: on the last day of the session in 1889, noted Bulloch, 'the police . . . were out in all their strength to defend the ladies seminaries of the city which our Bajan friends love to visit at this season'.[22] Student journalism is not a very reliable guide to this aspect of life, because it relied heavily on comic stereotypes. Just as all bajans were depicted as tender innocents straight from the nursery, so all senior medical students, especially the idle 'chronics', were supposed to be obsessed by their clothes and personal appearance, and to spend their leisure lounging in Union Street, ogling shopgirls and barmaids. But the medical reputation for rowdyism and dissipation was certainly not unearned.[23]

Singing, besides being popular before lectures, was an important part of most social occasions. The repertoire drew on a wide range, and varied according to fashion. From students' religious heritage came psalm tunes like the 'Old hundredth', to which the new revivalist hymn tunes were added. The American Civil War, when sympathies were with the north, saw much singing of 'John Brown's Body', and America also contributed what were then known as 'darkie' songs.[24] Neither Scottish nor British patriotic songs seem to have been particularly favoured, but comic songs from current theatrical hits were always popular, and there were standards like 'Abdul the Bulbul Ameer' and 'Mary had a little lamb' which lent themselves to ribald adaptation or pointed personal reference. Singing also figured, in a more refined form, at the formal dinners which were the most elaborate student occasions. Most classes held at least one 'class supper' in their lifetime, either before Christmas or at the end of the session. At these dinners, given in hotels and often with professors as guests, the standard forms of Victorian all-male sociability were followed, with a chairman and 'croupiers', a long toast-list, and a selection of solos by the more talented of the company, sometimes varied by recitations or musical performances. Comic songs were in order here too, but the main fare was the sentimental ballad, either Scottish in the lyric tradition of Burns or of the drawing-room type.

Annual dinners were also held by the various student societies, which provided the only regular diversion based on the university rather than the town. The two leading ones were taken over from King's College— the Debating (1848) and the Celtic (1854); the latter was chiefly a social organisation for Highland students, and conducted some of its business in Gaelic, but it also gave an important place to political debates. A Medical Society had false starts in 1865 and 1870, and did not become permanent until 1887.[25] The Literary Society started in 1871, but was for some years run by young graduates, admitting selected students by ballot. There were also some religious societies with a more specialised appeal, notably the Free Church Students' Association (1857), and the Missionary Association,

4 'Our reunion dinner' at the Grand Hotel, 28 December 1896. The bearded figure standing to reply to the toast of 'The Guests' is David Rennet, whose portrait had been presented that day. On his left at the head of the table is W L Mollison, chairman for the evening, and beyond him J Harrower, chairman of the Rennet Memorial Committee. The limelight photograph was taken by Messrs G & W Morgan. *Records of the Arts Class, 1868–72*, 3rd edn (Aberdeen, 1902), facing p. 119.

which went back to 1836. Societies normally met on Friday evenings at Marischal College, at staggered times so that individuals could attend more than one. This concentration of meetings on Friday persisted for many years, as did the winding-up of society activities in February, when students buckled down to examination revision. The basic formula was either a debate, or a paper presented by a member for general discussion; sometimes a professor was asked to inaugurate the session with an address—this became the custom at the Debating Society—but otherwise it was not usual to invite outside speakers, for the university societies reflected the contemporary pattern of study and self-improvement circles for young men.

The Debating Society was seen as the senior society, and organised a 'Grand Finale' in February, originally coinciding with bursary night, which was the high point of the student year. Originally simply a final meeting with speeches and the singing of 'Auld Lang Syne', from 1865 the finale included songs, musical solos, and recitations. The magistrands, who had formerly made humorous speeches taking leave of their *alma mater*, now took over 'Auld Lang Syne' as their special contribution. In 1867 drama was added, with the trial scene from *The Merchant of Venice*, using costumes borrowed from the Aberdeen theatre.[26] Extracts from Shakespeare remained popular for a few years, but in the 1870s they were replaced by short farces. In 1874, for example, 'the programme was extensive and varied, embracing vocal and instrumental music, character recitations, and dramatic representations. Two farces were put upon the stage, and all the parts were ably sustained.' In 1877 the programme was *Catch a Weasel* and *Ici on parle français*. In 1878 the performances moved from a classroom to the hall of Marischal College, and in 1879 they included 'a negro entertainment' and 'the Burlesque "Bombastes Furioso", which contained many local and university hits'. By 1885 the finale was popular enough to be moved to a public hall, the Silver Street Hall, the farces that year being *The Area Belle* and *Box and Cox*.[27] The dramatic tradition thus established was to have a long and almost continuous history. All the female parts were played by men, talents which were not always confined to the boards, for in the class of 1876: 'Diack and Jimmy Reid used to make up as girls with wonderful success, and were able to walk along the street (in the dusk) without attracting attention, although once I believe Reid excited suspicion and gathering up his skirts had to run for it. Our men rather affected histrionics'.[28]

The theatre was always popular, despite occasional attacks by the more rigid of the local clergy, and was one of the diversions offered by city life. Aberdeen's population grew from 74,000 in 1861 to 153,000 in 1901, and it acquired the forms of mass entertainment characteristic of industrial cities.[29] In the 1870s, Leask recalled the 'penny gaffs' and other predecessors of the music hall; the quayside area was then 'devoted to the wandering showman, the Cheap Jack, and the street singer'.[30] Whether students plunged lower in their search for pleasure is unrecorded. As a large port, Aberdeen certainly had its share of rough bars and brothels, and it would be surprising if students did not sometimes explore them. There are reports of students using brothels in Glasgow and Edinburgh,[31] and it seems unlikely that they differed from other middle-class youths of the time in seeking sexual experience from servants, shop assistants and other women in a vulnerable position. But the whole area of student sexuality remains a closed book: all that can be said with certainty is that it occupied a good deal more space in students' minds and imaginations than it can in this study. It is also probable that Aberdeen students, with their rural back-grounds and conventional religious upbringing, had particular difficulty in coping with the emotional demands of adulthood, adjusting to the expanded horizons which a university education revealed, and accepting the challenge of new and radical ideas. But if the sources do not allow us to reconstruct the inner life of students, they do at least show what intellectual, cultural and political experiences were available for them to choose from.

The concentrated character of arts teaching gave professors a strong personal influence over students. For many of those with academic tastes, Aberdeen was above all a classical university, and in the first year students encountered William Geddes, nicknamed 'Homer', professor of Greek from 1860 until 1885, when he became principal. His scholarship seems to have made a deep impression, and there was a Hellenic Society which was really a study group of senior pupils meeting at his house. The most celebrated of the professors was Alexander Bain, professor of logic from 1860 to 1880, an Aberdeen man who had begun life as a handloom weaver. Students met Bain twice, since his chair also covered the teaching of English in the first year. As a philosopher, he was noted as a disciple of Mill and Comte and a religious agnostic. He avoided controversy in his lectures, but his general intellectual stance challenged the religious orthodoxy of the age, which was under attack simultaneously from Darwinism, following the publication of the *Origin of Species* in 1859, and from the new biblical criticism coming from Germany. Darwinist ideas, and materialist explanations of life in general, were strongly championed by John Struthers, professor of anatomy and the dominant figure in the medical school, while the natural history class, a compulsory part of the MA curriculum, covered the two subjects of zoology and geology which were at the forefront of science's challenge to religion.

The challenge was countered by William Martin, professor of moral philosophy, who attempted to refute Bain and remained loyal to the Scottish 'common sense' school of philosophy which justified religious belief in rational terms, and to the doctrines of natural religion expressed in Butler's *Analogy*. But Martin was a figure of fun, who was unable to keep order in class and was mercilessly ragged by his students, not least on the subject of his very obvious wig; Martin retired in 1876, but his successor, John Fyfe, had the same old-fashioned philosophical views. The cause of religion was also strengthened by the lectures on Christian evidences. William Bruce, a student of the 1860s who later entered the church, remembered these as a steadying influence, and they did not dodge the problems, for Renan's *Life of Jesus*, translated in 1864 and a product of the new philological scholarship, was one of the subjects tackled.[32]

From the first year onwards, therefore, students were exposed to new ideas. As Bruce recalled in his capacity as editor of the 1864 class record, 'King's was no cloistered College, for the great currents of literary and political life flowed through it. We felt their flow, and began even then to find our aptitudes and shape our future'.[33] One who felt those flows acutely was the biblical scholar William Robertson Smith, perhaps the most famous student of the 1860s. Robertson Smith's father was Free Church minister of Keig, a rural Aberdeenshire parish; there he educated his own children along with a handful of boarders from similar families. In 1861 Robertson Smith and his brother George went to the university, sharing lodgings with a sister who was also pursuing her education. William was 15 and George 14—the youngest students of their year—and they had won bursaries of £30 and £10 respectively.[34] Both the sister, in 1864, and George, immediately after graduating brilliantly in 1866, were to die of consumption—a fate which overcame all too many students in fact as well as fiction. While the Smith brothers were students, the details of university life and the ideas which they encountered in Bain's classes and elsewhere were relayed in letters home, and eagerly discussed during the vacations. University friends were frequent visitors at the manse, including Robertson Nicoll, the son of a neighbouring minister.[35] The Free manse of Keig can be seen as a symbol of the older Scottish culture, in which clergymen and teachers diffused university influence and intellectual cultivation throughout the rural society in which the university had its roots. But Smith's own pursuit of truth was to undermine that culture's religious foundations: he became professor at the Free Church College in Aberdeen, but his use of the new critical methods eventually led to a celebrated series of heresy trials and to his resignation.

This was therefore an unusually interesting period, when the intellectual conflicts of the age were played out within the compulsory Aberdeen curriculum, and when the religious background of Aberdeen students put them at the sharp end of the debate, not necessarily destroying their faith, but forcing them to rethink it. Some reacted more strongly, as the brief history of the Ethical Society shows. This was founded in 1883 for 'free religious discussions—these not being allowed in any of the existing societies. Those interested at the start were more or less hostile to current views on religion'. In its first session it discussed such topics as disestablishment, miracles, poverty, and the religion of the Hebrews. Its leaders were Gordon Beveridge, a medical student, and P C Mitchell, a minister's son who reacted against his upbringing; introduced to Darwin in the natural history class, he became a professional zoologist. The society met in a cafe on Sunday evenings rather than in a university room, since the university authorities were unsympathetic. An address from Bain was to have opened the society's second session, but it collapsed in 1884 because of internal dissensions between the moderates and the 'Extreme Left' led by Mitchell.[36]

The university societies encouraged intellectual debate, but did little to develop cultural tastes. There was no teaching of music or art in the university, and though a University Choral Society was formed in 1875, there were perennial complaints that students failed to participate in the city's musical life. For most students the main cultural influence was English literature, especially after Bain was succeeded by William Minto, who was more interested in the literary than the philosophical side of his chair (there was no separate English chair until 1894). Minto was the most popular of the arts professors in the 1880s, until his early death. Having been a successful journalist and critic, he came 'fresh from the great world of London', and gave students a sense of personal contact with the luminaries of contemporary literature.[37] As a student in the 1860s, Minto had been one of the frequenters of the Free manse of Keig, and as a young assistant in the 1870s was a mainstay of the select Literary Society, along with Robertson Nicoll. Their taste ran to Tennyson, Swinburne and George Eliot, but the average student probably stuck to the older classics.[38]

The Debating Society also discussed literary and historical subjects. Its constitution banned religious questions, including church politics, which in Scotland were a large part of party politics; but otherwise its political interests ranged widely, over both foreign and domestic questions. The former included serfdom in Russia, the American Civil War, contemporary events in Italy, and (in the 1870s) republicanism versus monarchy in France. Domestic issues included the organisation of education, the case of Governor Eyre and the Jamaican rebellion (1866), the 'recent Reform agitation' (1867), the abolition of the House of Lords, the franchise for women, Gladstone versus Disraeli, the Irish question, and compulsory military service (a surprisingly regular topic). There were also debates on questions of university reform, and on rather hackneyed general or moral questions such as capital punishment, blood sports, the morality of the stage, or the press versus the pulpit as influences on public opinion; at the end of the session there was usually a comic debate (tea versus toddy, married versus single life).[39]

Some of these themes were the conventional rhetorical ones of traditional essay writing, and there was also an element of convention in the politics. In the age of Gladstone, a serious young man was expected to take an informed interest in politics and foreign affairs just as he was expected to go to church, or to read Macaulay, Carlyle, and the heavier novelists. But it is also the case that in the age of Gladstone middle-class political culture was particularly lively, and as with religious questions the background of Aberdeen students sensitised them to the political agenda of liberalism; it was a creed of small towns and independent producers, and the North East was one of its electoral strongholds. The Highland students seem to have had particularly radical views, and there were vigorous political debates in the Celtic Society. In 1873 it was debating whether sheep-farming or deer-forests did more injury to the Highlands, and in the 1880s, when Highland issues were prominent in Scottish politics, it ranged over such questions as landlordism and the nationalisation of land, home rule, disestablishment of the church, and public versus private enterprise.[40]

The liberal inclinations of students at this time are reflected in the history of rectorial elections. Under the 1858 Act, the rector was elected by the students; in principle, he chaired the Court, the university's governing body, and appointed an assessor who also sat there. Before 1858, only Marischal College and Glasgow possessed student-elected rectors. Glasgow had usually chosen nationally-known politicians or literary figures, who appeared once to give an inaugural address but otherwise did nothing; the 'ornamental' rector also became the norm at Edinburgh and St Andrews, and contests were usually on strict party lines. But at Marischal it had been more common to choose local MPs or peers, who sometimes took a direct interest in university affairs, and something of this tradition was carried over.

The first election was in 1860. Aberdeen students voted indirectly through four 'nations', defined by birthplaces, which elected procurators who in turn chose the rector. This could easily lead to a tie, in which case the chancellor had the casting vote. In 1860 a tie duly occurred, and since there was no chancellor in office his vote was exercised by the principal. The candidates were the Liberal lawyer Edward Maitland and Sir Andrew Leith Hay, a former Liberal MP. But the contest was complicated by the old King's and Marischal rivalry, and by tension between students and professors: Hay had been put forward as a local man who would chair the Court in person and defend students' interests, while Maitland was the favoured professorial candidate.[41] Principal Campbell, a King's man, voted for Maitland although Hay had received more student votes. This provoked great indignation, and 'the most rowdy proceedings that ever characterised the installation of a Rector at Aberdeen'[42] when Maitland gave his inaugural address before 600 students in 1861. Uproar drowned all the proceedings, including the opening prayer and a formal protest by the Hay party; missiles were thrown, including dried peas, sticks, and broken pieces of the wooden forms in the hall, and one splinter drew blood on Maitland's face. The noisiest students were ejected, but they then threw stones through the windows and eventually stormed the hall again. Maitland finally managed to make himself heard, and was able to finish his address in comparative peace. The police were outside the hall, but no arrests were made, despite the indignation and embarrassment felt by the professors. Rowdyism on this scale was disapproved of by public opinion, but there was a tradition of licensed disorder at rectorials to which this incident gave new life.

In 1863 the politician Lord Russell was elected, against another Liberal, the MP for Elgin Burghs, Mountstuart Grant Duff. In 1866 Duff was the successful candidate, and his inaugural address put forward a programme of university reform, championing modern subjects and attacking the dominance of the classics; he followed this up by taking the chair at Court meetings.[43] At this time discontent with the curriculum was widely felt, and was expressed especially through the General Council, a statutory body consisting in theory of all graduates, and in practice of professional men in Aberdeen who had the time and interest to attend its meetings. Change was opposed by the majority of the Senatus, led by 'Homer' Geddes: compulsory Greek was a special target of the reformers, and Geddes published a refutation of Duff in 1869.[44] Since both Senatus and General Council elected assessors to the Court, the body which had authority to change the curriculum, the rector and his assessor occupied a crucial position, and both the conservative professors and the reforming minority led by Bain and Struthers took sides in rectorial elections (or, it could be said, used them to fight their own battles). In 1869 Duff stood again, and Sir William Stirling Maxwell, author, scholar and former Conservative MP, was put up against him. Duff had the majority of votes, but there was again a tie between the nations, and when the chancellor cast his vote for Maxwell the events of 1860–1 threatened to repeat themselves, until Maxwell resolved the situation by resigning. At a re-run election, Duff was elected with only nominal opposition. His second address, devoted to 'The changes most wanted in Aberdeen University', once more put the case for science, modern languages, history and other new subjects.

During his second term, Duff attended only 9 out of 31 Court meetings, but in 1872 he proposed a comprehensive reform of the arts curriculum. As his successor, student reformers first put forward Charles Darwin, which provoked a lively correspondence in the local press after a fierce attack on Darwin's 'infidelity'.[45] Darwin declined, but was replaced by his disciple T H Huxley, the foremost champion of scientific education in Britain, and no less of an infidel. A professor's daughter recollected that:

> feeling ran tremendously high and we children were strongly infected by it. Being the daughter of a theological professor I looked upon Huxley as a most dangerous and perversive influence. My great friend, a daughter of Professor Struthers, espoused his cause very warmly, and well do I remember the joy with which we hailed the students sporting the colours of our choice.[46]

Huxley saw himself as carrying on Duff's work, and his address on 'Universities actual and ideal' (not given until 1874) was a classic statement of the case for modern education. He attended six out of ten possible Court meetings, concentrating on reform of the medical curriculum, with the support of Struthers and the medical students.

Conflict between Courts, General Councils and Senates was characteristic of all the Scottish universities at this time, and led to a royal commission in 1876, of which Huxley was a prominent member. It is perhaps not surprising that Aberdeen professors giving evidence complained about the rectorial system and wanted to reduce student influence on the Court, especially as according to one professor 'but a short time ago there was an idea amongst the students that they would elect a Rector from their own number'.[47] However this may be (and there is no other evidence for it), the heat went out of the issue for a time, and the next two elections were for the first time purely party-political, resulting in the election of the Liberals W E Forster in 1875 and Lord Rosebery in 1878. In these political contests, the nation which contained the English students was consistently the most Conservative, while those representing the rural hinterland were usually Liberal.

In 1881 controversy returned. Alexander Bain had recently retired from his chair, and had been defeated in a contest for one of the General Council seats on the Court. His partisans now put him forward for the rectorship, and he was elected by a large majority. Once more, the professors did not conceal their hostility. Bain's anti-religious views and strong Liberal politics made him a contentious figure, and an unsuccessful attempt was made to unseat him on the grounds that retired professors were ineligible. When he gave his address in 1882, the occasion proved the most turbulent since 1861. There was continual noise from bagpipes, trumpets, hooters and other improvised instruments, and fireworks were thrown as well as dried peas. After about half an hour, Bain abandoned his speech. He proved an assiduous rector, attending every meeting of the Court except one. He took up the struggle against Greek, and supported the medical students in their perennial complaints about the curriculum. In 1883 they won a notable victory in a dispute over examinations in pathology: Bain used his casting vote in the Court in favour of the students, who had made a formal legal appeal against the decision of the Senatus.[48] Bain was re-elected in 1884, against Lord Randolph Churchill, but wisely abstained from giving a second address.

By the next rectorial contest in 1887, as we shall see, an attempt was made to avoid disorders. But as time went by, the events surrounding the elections tended to expand. Once a candidate had agreed to stand, he played no personal part in the election, but his supporters threw themselves into activity:

WISDOM & WINDBAGS

PROF. STRUTHERS.   REV. PROF. TRAIL.   PROF. MINTO.   PROF. BAIN AND
                                                                          LORD R. CHURCHILL,

5   The Rectorial contest of 1884 in a contemporary cartoon. P J Anderson,
ed., *Rectorial Addresses delivered in the Universities of Aberdeen, 1835–1900*
(Aberdeen, 1902), facing p. 383.

> Class work is tabooed—committee work takes its place; the attire of the
> student is adorned with party-coloured rosettes—his lady-love quickly fol-
> lowing suit; the orators and wits of the Class betake themselves to the
> platform and to the printing offices; and a deluge of literature—more spicy
> than select, more humorous than academic—is hurled at the electorate.[49]

Sometimes the parties published full-length magazines, and there were
always cartoons, posters, and 'squibs'—usually spoof versions of playbills
or local newspapers. The election proper began with the nomination
meeting, which was followed by a ritual fight or 'battle for the standard'.
After this, as in 1872, 'the students formed themselves into a procession
and marched through some of the principal streets of the city with the
usual demonstrations. They visited the houses of some of the Professors,
giving free vent to their feelings'.[50] Such visits were an established practice,
and P C Mitchell recalled the usefulness of a tin-can-and-string device for
'torchlight processions, rectorial elections, and demonstrations outside the
houses of unpopular professors'.[51] Popular ones were also visited and given
a cheer.

Another procession accompanied the rectorial address, which was trans-
ferred from Marischal College to Aberdeen's largest public hall, the Music
Hall. As students marched down Union Street, they threw peasemeal and
other missiles at each other and at respectable citizens; tradesmen's vehicles,
buses and trams were regarded as fair game. Peasemeal was a particular
favourite on all such occasions: it was made up in small paper bags which
burst on impact, covering the targets in a dense yellow cloud. At Grant
Duff's address in 1870, for example, 'the fun became fast and furious';
Duff's words were drowned by singing, horns, bells and rattles, and 'the
Professors, whether on the platform with the Rector or in the arena among
the peasemeal warriors, were spared no indignity that triumphant anarchy
could inflict'.[52] The peasemeal flew especially thickly at Rosebery's inaug-
uration in 1880, and the management of the Music Hall, who must have
dreaded these three-yearly occasions, made the banning of peasemeal a
condition in 1882. Another feature of the Rosebery inaugural was the
torchlight procession. These had been known before—Robertson Smith
participated in one in 1863, probably to celebrate the Prince of Wales's
wedding—but this seems to have been the beginning of their association
with rectorials.[53]

These manifestations allowed the release of youthful high spirits in a
collective context where punishment was impossible, but they also had
the character of an accepted tradition. Similar disorder, though of a more
good-humoured kind, was customary at the annual graduation ceremony,
despite its being held in King's College Chapel; even the principal's prayers
and sermon were interrupted by ribaldry and songs, and 'a perfect fusillade
of running jokes and humorous sallies had to be endured' by the graduands
as they were capped.[54] Licensed disorder on ritual occasions is characteristic
of societies where authority and discipline are normally strong, and it is
understandable that for Aberdeen students, who came from communities
where respect for parents, teachers and ministers was strongly enforced,
and the expression of emotion was inhibited, a chance to defy and even
humiliate the professors, and mock the symbols of authority, had a cath-
artic effect.

For many students rectorials were an excuse for larking about and
fighting, but their political significance should not be underestimated.
These elections were unique in being a statutory procedure which gave
the vote to men (and women after 1892) before the age of 21, and they
provided an apprenticeship in adult politics. After 1868, indeed, when the
university franchise was extended to Scotland, those students who were
already MAs had a parliamentary vote. But the distinctive feature of
Aberdeen in the 1870s and 1880s was the role of the rectorship in questions
of university reform, the division on which largely corresponded with
that between critics and defenders of religion. The immediate result was

confrontation with the conservative professoriate, but the way was prepared for the more permanent and consensual institution of the Students' Representative Council, part of the wider development of student life and corporate feeling which will be discussed in the next chapter.

Chapter 2

The Corporate Ideal

In all the Scottish universities, the 1880s saw the establishment of Students' Representative Councils, the beginning of regular student journals, an expansion of the activity of societies, and—except at Aberdeen, where this was delayed—the building of student unions. University sport too became firmly established, though it had earlier roots. This growth of corporate life was an international phenomenon: the pioneers in Aberdeen were very conscious of being part of a movement, and in its early years the magazine *Alma Mater* had frequent reports on developments in France, Germany or the United States. Their experience was more relevant than the English example of a residential, conspicuously expensive and socially exclusive student life. Thus although elements of 'anglicisation' were present—one symptom being the adoption of the term 'Varsity', which remained normal throughout our period—there was little direct imitation of Oxford or Cambridge.

Though the residential idea failed to win over student opinion, it did have some advocates. In 1870 the General Council passed a motion calling for 'rooms within the College for board, lodging, and common study', and set up a committee to study proposals for a residential hall, as had existed at St Andrews since 1861. If run commercially it would have to charge £50 a session, which would exclude poorer students; but fees could be lower if the building itself was already paid for, and an appeal was launched. This failed, but the issue was still being aired before the royal commission of 1876. Principal Campbell stressed the 'extreme desirableness' of a Common Hall, where the students could 'assemble in the evenings free from temptation', have access to a library and tutorial help, 'and where, especially, there would be some opportunity for the rustic class of students learning to use their knife and fork: in fact, for their learning the usages of society, by which a number of the young men from the country destined in after-life to move in the sphere of gentlemen would be greatly benefited'.[1]

This desire to mould 'gentlemen' reflected, as has already been suggested, the need to compete with the products of English public schools and universities in the professions and public services. Social as well as academic qualifications were now required, and the issue came up in practical form over the Indian Civil Service, an important Aberdeen outlet. New regulations in the 1870s tried to insist that candidates should spend their university career in residential accommodation, which would have excluded Aberdeen students altogether; the University Court fought hard to get this modified, and had to agree in 1878 that candidates would lodge with one of the professors so that their conduct could be supervised. In 1884 the regulation was relaxed, but there were still thoughts at that time of setting up a hall for these students.[2]

Campbell's successor, Pirie, was also interested in knife-and-fork education, inaugurating an annual 'breakfast' for magistrands in a city hotel, where toasts were drunk in tea and coffee, and professors' wives were present.[3] Otherwise social contacts between professors and students outside the classroom were rare. Professors might entertain prizemen or favoured honours students in their homes, but otherwise it was considered a sign of affability if they recognised their students on the street. Some professors like Bain, though respected, were notoriously angular in their social relations; perhaps those who had humble origins were especially conscious of their dignity. Most professors in any case took the view that the private lives and extra-curricular activities of students were not their business. By contrast with the paternalism of Oxford and Cambridge, or the political controls found in many continental countries, the Scottish universities made no attempt to supervise student societies, newspapers or debates, or to extend discipline beyond the maintenance of order in the classrooms and university precincts. The reverse side of this was that the development of corporate life received little official encouragement or financial support. In 1880, it is true, the university drew up a list of desiderata for the attention of potential benefactors, which was published for some years in the *Calendar*. These included such measures for 'the physical comfort and humanising culture of the Students' as a gymnasium and recreation ground, a 'room for refreshments' at King's, and a dining hall 'where Students could obtain a comfortable meal singly or together'. But benefactors were slow to appear, and the students themselves had to take the initiative.

One early symptom of change was the revival of student journalism— there had been magazines before the fusion, but none in the 1860s. In 1872 there was a single number of the *Medical Students' Shaver*, a humorous publication, and this was followed in the 1872–3 session by the much more serious *Aberdeen Medical Student*. Many of its articles were of a strictly medical kind, but it also aimed to 'chronicle the events of the student life of the session', and covered the 1872 rectorial, giving strong support to Huxley. It also reflected the growth of athletics, with especially full football reports. A leader on physical education stressed the value of sport as a counter to overwork and 'grinding' (excessive study), and claimed that a gymnasium would be more use than 'the caste-mongering College Hall that has been so long before the General Council', and 'might lead to the developement [*sic*] of some pleasant phases of student social life, a thing at present without existence here, unless, indeed, you can call by that name an occasional "meet" for a fierce dissipation'.[4] In 1873 the magazine extended its appeal to arts students, becoming the *Aberdeen University Gazette*. An editorial on 'Muscular Christianity' endorsed English ideas of physical education, but a residential hall was still condemned: 'What student among us is prepared to give up the freedom and comfort of his lodgings for the doubtful advantage to be derived from eating his meals under the auspices of the University?' But the *Gazette* was not against 'a room set apart for conversation, beer, and music', to attract students away from public houses, and one article argued that Aberdeen students needed more social polish, including the removal of provincialisms from their speech: 'if they lived more together, more in public, a higher tone of morality and manners would result, and outsiders would look on our graduates as, in the highest sense, gentlemen'.[5]

At this point *Life in a Northern University* was published. One contributor thought it 'a book overflowing with the most undiluted sentimental twaddle that has been written for many a long day', but the reviewer found it 'a faithful and vivid record', valuable in showing that Aberdeen students were not as boorish as was supposed, and that even here university life was 'a powerful force ceaselessly moulding and fitting us for the Battle of Life. The humanizing influence of contact with each other in our rooms, in our classes, and in our societies, contributes to the formation of the cultured gentleman more than the mere brand M.A.'.[6] Thus the ideal of the gentleman was powerful in student as well as professorial circles, though it was to be achieved in a non-residential context.

The *Gazette* lasted only one session, as did *The Academic* of 1877–8. This was edited by Leask, and had a more literary flavour, with little comment on current events, though it too called for a greater 'social element' in student life.[7] In 1883, however, *Alma Mater* began its long life.[8] At first its finances were fragile, but they were secure once local tradesmen began to advertise regularly. *Alma* appeared weekly until February, when most university social activities ceased, and from 1889 had two or three summer numbers. A rival appeared in 1897, *College Chimes*, but this did not survive

6   The mastheads used for many years in *Alma Mater*'s gossip columns.
'They haif said: Quhat say thay: let thame say' was the motto of George
Keith, 5th Earl Marischal and founder of Marischal College.

beyond its first number. The format of *Alma* soon settled to a fixed pattern:
a leader or two on current questions, separate columns of news and gossip
for King's and Marischal, short stories and poetry, and reports on sport,
student societies, and the theatre. Profiles of professors, not always uncriti-
cal, were a popular feature, and in the early years the King's and Marischal
columns were filled with their sayings and doings, or with incidents from
the classroom. The literary content varied according to the tastes of the
editor, but there was never any shortage of verse. Bulloch, a prolific
contributor to the paper, wrote a hundred 'College Carols' on student life
or topical matters; after graduating he became a sub-editor on the Aberdeen *Free Press*, but continued to write for *Alma* until he left in 1893 for
London, where he eventually became editor of the *Graphic*. For *Alma*
fitted into a journalistic as well as a university context: in this golden age
for the provincial press, Aberdeen had three morning papers, and two
social and literary journals, the *Northern Figaro* and *Bon Accord*, all of which
reported university affairs fully for their middle-class readers. Like *Alma*,
they contributed to a flow of Aberdeen men to Fleet Street which was
already legendary.

Alma Mater was at first run by the Debating Society, which was attempting to meet the growing need for a representative organisation—it was this society, for example, which negotiated cheap Christmas tickets with the railway companies. Soon this gap was filled by the Students' Representative Council, whose origins, however, were not in Aberdeen. From 1881 Scottish university reform bills came before Parliament regularly, and students needed to find a common voice if they were to have any say in this process. They were also influenced by developments abroad, and it was after a visit to Germany that Robert Fitzroy Bell founded the SRC at Edinburgh in 1884. At Aberdeen the Debating Society took the first steps, and the SRC was formed in the last weeks of 1884, with the encouragement of Bain as rector. St Andrews and Glasgow followed in 1885. In 1888 the SRCs held their first joint conference at Aberdeen, and the 'Inter-Universities Conference' became an important annual meeting at which ideas on the development of student life were exchanged. Students were thus able to have some influence on the Universities (Scotland) Act of 1889, and on the commissioners' Ordinances which followed it. The act itself gave some official recognition to the SRCs by empowering the rector to consult them before appointing his assessor, and it became normal at Aberdeen for him to respect their wishes; assessors were usually local business or professional men, who served under more than one rector. But the 1889 Act did not extend student representation, even though the size of the Court was increased, nor did the SRC establish, like the General Council, a statutory right to be consulted about changes.

Still, there was plenty of work for the SRC within the university. It was financed at first by a voluntary levy on students, and composed of delegates from the different years and faculties, a system taken over from the Debating Society; the president and other officers were elected by the delegates, not directly. The first council was presided over by Patrick Rattray, a medical student who had taken the initiative in its foundation, and included three future professors—H J C Grierson, Ashley Mackintosh, and Robert McKerron. Medical students were always especially active in the SRC, and presidents were often men in their late twenties, who were already MAs. The medical curriculum was a constant source of complaints, and dealing with them was part of the SRC's routine work, along with grievances about examinations, the bursary competition, the library, the state of the buildings, or the absence of social facilities.

At first, being conceived at the time of Bain's rectorship and the pathology affair, the SRC enjoyed strained relations with the university authorities. In 1887 *Alma Mater* criticised its confrontational approach, and suggested that it would win more support if it became the organising body for all student activities, advice which was heeded.[9] In 1887 societies were given direct representation on the council (until 1895), and in 1888 the SRC took over *Alma Mater*. It developed various useful services, including a lodgings register, a book exchange and a Students' Handbook which appeared annually from 1893. Even so, interesting the mass of students in the SRC's work was not easy, and in 1892, as retiring president, Ashley Mackintosh 'lamented the lack of University-life amongst Students, and the meagre interest displayed by them in the welfare of their own University and of other Universities throughout the world'.[10] In the 1890s SRC elections became more lively with the development of 'heckling meetings', where candidates addressed their constituents. But these were often occasions for facetiousness and rowdyism, especially in the first year, where they became set occasions for older students to rag the bajans and the 'lambs' (their medical equivalents). SRC elections were often followed by bills from the university for damage to classrooms.

One of the first functions of the Edinburgh SRC had been to maintain order and eliminate rowdyism during the tercentenary ceremonies of 1884 and at rectorial addresses. At Aberdeen, the disorder at Bain's address in 1882 was vividly remembered, and if repeated was likely to discredit the new claims of the student body. In 1887 the rectorial election was a political one. Lord Randolph Churchill's candidacy in 1884 had encouraged the formation of a Conservative Association, which seems to have been the first student political organisation at Aberdeen. In 1887 its candidate was the Chancellor of the Exchequer, George Goschen, who defeated the Liberal John Morley by a substantial majority. This reflected the split in the Liberal party over Irish home rule, and the Irish issue featured in the rectorial campaign, though there was also some feeling that electing Goschen would loosen the Treasury's purse-strings at a time when Aberdeen was seeking a grant for new buildings. The political crisis of 1886 and the establishment of Liberal Unionism seem to have led to a permanent shift in political allegiances: where formerly Liberalism had been unchallenged, political activities and rectorial election results henceforth showed a more equal balance. The Conservative Association itself was as much a social as a political organisation, with smoking and reading rooms near Marischal; it moved to a larger set in 1888, but by 1891 was said to be inactive, and by 1892 had disappeared.[11] This spasmodic existence was to be characteristic of political clubs, which often came into being only for rectorial campaigns.

In 1888, when Goschen came to give his address, the Senatus was only too happy to hand over responsibility for keeping order to the SRC, which now allocated the seating and provided stewards. It also issued a three-part warning to students: there was to be no prior procession to the

Music Hall; sticks, fireworks, peas, peasemeal, flour and trumpets were banned; and anyone 'conducting himself in a way unbecoming a student and a gentleman' would be ejected and handed over to the Senatus for rustication.[12] These arrangements worked, and Goschen received a peaceful hearing. The delegation of management to the SRC continued, and was later extended to graduation ceremonies. But the next rectorial address, in 1891, was marked by the 'carriage affair'. After Lord Huntly had spoken, his carriage was unyoked and students drew him to his hotel. Then 'those in charge of the carriage dragged the vehicle, with a number of their comrades seated inside, through the principal streets. At the harbour they came into conflict with the police, and in a slight *melée* that occurred the students threatened to pitch the vehicle into the dock'.[13] Eventually they smashed it up while trying to get it into Marischal, to the disgust of Bulloch: 'Here is the good name of Aberdeen students, which the Representative Council, & Alma Mater has been trying to build up for years, blown to atoms by the work of a few cads in half an hour. I hope they will suffer'. The SRC did indeed condemn this 'dastardly act of Vandalism' and helped to identify the culprits, who were reprimanded by the Senatus.[14] The effect of the affair on public opinion was shown later in the year, when the local MP Peter Esslemont compared it to some Irish election riots, causing much offence to the students. Also dissatisfied was the carriage proprietor, who submitted a bill for £55. An appeal to the students responsible failed, and only a personal advance of £25 from Principal Geddes prevented the hirer from taking action against Huntly himself.[15] The 'carriage affair' was still rumbling on in 1892, and severely embarrassed the SRC. It showed that responsibility had its disadvantages, for the council could now be blamed—and sent bills—by irate citizens who suffered from student actions over which the SRC had no real control.

Damage to property was to be repeated, and few rectorial addresses were to be as quiet as Goschen's. Noise of all kinds remained usual at the address, but the SRC strategy successfully diverted other forms of disorder to two occasions when the rector himself was safely absent, the battle for the standard after the nomination meeting, and the torchlight procession on the evening of the election. Marches and peasemeal were now confined to the nomination battle. The supporters of each party formed up in the town and marched to Marischal with their standard behind a pipe band, pelting buildings and passers-by with peasemeal; in the quadrangle, with an audience including ladies and professors, the battle followed a set procedure and was refereed by the sacrists. In these tussles the 'football men' were prominent, and football jerseys, as well as jackets turned inside out, gave some protection from the peasemeal, flour or soot. Once one of the standards had been captured, it was again paraded through the town, and the day ended with a night at the theatre.[16] The indulgence of the

7 'Students' Rectorial fight', 1896, from a painting by H Giles. It may be compared with the photograph of 1902 (Plate 17). P J Anderson, ed., *Rectorial Addresses delivered in the Universities of Aberdeen, 1835–1900* (Aberdeen, 1902), facing p. 390.

authorities towards these events did not go unremarked by the city's working-class youth: 'Some amusement was caused the other day when three or four street Arabs up before the Baillie, for disturbing the lieges, explained that they had been "fighting for their standard". The Baillie let them off'.[17]

The torchlight procession, now a popular spectacle for the Aberdeen public, also took on a standard form. From 1890 fancy dress was worn, female costumes of all kinds being especially popular. The procession through the main streets was led by mounted police officials, and the municipality co-operated by turning off the street lights. The military authorities played their part by allowing the procession to end in the courtyard of Castlehill barracks, where the torches were thrown onto a bonfire. A local journalist described the scene in 1893:

> Joining hands, the 500 students, to the accompaniment of a vigorous tom-tom on the big drum, executed a sort of general war dance round the blazing pile. Suddenly this ceased, and the dance was taken up by couples, who, in

waltz and polka, whirled round and round to the strains of the bagpipes. The picture was at once weird and droll in the extreme.

Many threw their fancy dress on the fire, and 'a host of the sultans and mandarins, priests and pirates, disappeared from the scene, their places being taken by staid looking young men clad in homely Scotch tweeds'; but others 'masqueraded in their novel attire until the night was far spent'.[18]

Lord Huntly was elected rector in 1890, and twice re-elected. He was a local nobleman who had been Huxley's opponent in 1872, but although he was a Unionist, and was opposed on each occasion by a Liberal, he was put forward as a non-political or 'working' rector who would take a close interest in university affairs. This movement was especially supported by Bulloch, who put the case for it as editor of *Alma Mater* in 1890–1 and in a pamphlet on the history of the rectorship, which made much of the institution's mediaeval origins, arguing that students were foolish to throw away their real influence in the university by voting for London politicians like Goschen.[19] Huntly lived up to expectations, chairing most of the Court meetings during his term, and was clearly very popular.

One delicate affair which he had to handle was the case of David Johnston, professor of biblical criticism. Johnston was an Orkney minister appointed by the Crown in 1893. His lectures proved unpopular, partly because they were unmethodical and confused, partly because of Johnston's refusal to deal with the New Testament and his unfamiliarity with modern scholarship. Student protest was expressed at first through classroom disorder, but formal complaints were also made, and though the University Court was reluctant to act, a series of inquiries ended in 1896 with Johnston being required to resign. He had alienated opinion by launching public attacks on his students as 'miscreants'. But legal difficulties in arranging a pension allowed him to stay in office, and in 1897 he gave a provocative opening lecture at Marischal. Though there were only 20 students in the divinity faculty—the Johnston affair had exacerbated its decline—this lecture was attended by over a hundred, and had to be abandoned amid shouting, singing, and jeering. It ended with a pitched battle between arts and medical students, and a procession down Union Street. The Senatus made other arrangements for teaching biblical criticism, and in 1898, when it refused to allow Johnston to use Marischal College, he gave his opening lecture on private premises, with a police guard.[20] The affair ended in 1899 with Johnston's death. He was a man of marked personal eccentricity, and his appointment was evidently a mistake and a personal tragedy. But the case illustrated both the growing propensity of students to rowdyism, and their ability to complain effectively if the necessity arose. On a much smaller scale, the conduct of his class by the Latin professor, W M Ramsay, caused complaint on more than one occasion, and there was a minor crisis

8 'The Shinty Club, 1910–11'. Back row (left to right) G A C Gordon, C Tighe, J D Pratt, A G Maclean, L W Bain, J Rose; middle row, D Mackenzie, K Maclennan, D N Lowe, A Skinner, A Macaulay; front, F R Cramb, V C Macrae. A shinty club had existed before 1860, but had lapsed, and this team represents one of its subsequent revivals. *Alma Mater* says that most members of the team had never played before, and hopes 'that students who don't play any other game at the 'Varsity will become members of the Shinty club'. *AM, Athletic Album* 1910–11, pp. xxvii and xxxviii.

in 1901 when the editorial committee of *Alma* was suspended by the SRC for publishing an attack on him.[21] It is a myth, therefore, that students in the past were docile beings who did not question academic decisions, for both *Alma* and the SRC took a close interest in the curriculum, the quality of the teaching, and on occasion the merits of rival candidates for chairs.

For the origins of student athleticism we must go back to W M Ramsay's student days. Even before 1860, students had discharged their energies in cricket, football and other games, but there had been little formal organisation, though a cricket club is recorded at Marischal in 1849. The Highland game of shinty had a club at King's before 1860, and a University Shinty Club was formed in 1861, but this did not last.[22] By the 1860s team games were becoming popular among middle-class youth generally; in Scotland this movement began in Edinburgh secondary schools, but soon spread to Aberdeen as to other towns.[23] The pioneering local school was the Gymnasium, and its students (including Ramsay) became the leaders of university sport. English medical students, some of them from public schools, also brought 'great energy in organising games, and a good sporting tradition'.[24] For this was a field where English students made a more distinctive contribution than in other aspects of the student movement. The activists of the SRC, for example, tended to come from middle-class Aberdeen families. Off the athletic field, Englishmen were noted chiefly for their comparative wealth and indolence, and their habit of saying 'Y-ah' instead of 'Yes'.[25]

University sport began as a branch of the sporting activity of the city, not a direct imitation of English habits. The history of cricket illustrates this. The game became well established in the 1850s, and the Aberdeen Cricket Club, founded in 1857 and renamed the Aberdeenshire in 1867, became the premier club of the North East; but there were many others in the city and outside, and by the late 1880s the Aberdeenshire Cricket Association included over twenty clubs.[26] At the Gymnasium, the Chanonry House Cricket Club was in existence by 1858, and also supervised football and other games, the Gymnasium being the first school to have its own pitch.[27] In the university, despite the absence of many students after April, there were cricket clubs at both King's and Marischal in the 1870s and 1880s. In 1883, for example, the King's club was renting its own field, and played Ellon, Stonehaven, and Banchory as well as city clubs like the Aberdeenshire, the two Grammar Schools, Chanonry House, and the Royal Lunatic Asylum (staff rather than inmates). Ellon was visited again in 1884: 'the return journey, of which the most salient feature was a prolonged stoppage at a half-way-house, will long be remembered as one of the most delightful events of the King's season'. This journey was by break, but railways now made such visits easier, though they might still have an air of ceremony: when the King's club went to Oldmeldrum in 1889, they were met at the station by the town band.[28] Thus university teams were part of the local cricket scene, and inter-university matches were uncommon. *Ad hoc* 'Aberdeen University' XIs appeared to play opponents like the Aberdeenshire, and in 1886 a University Cricket Club was formed which played five matches, including one with Edinburgh University. But the King's and Marischal clubs continued, and until the university had its own ground, students were just as likely to play for the Aberdeenshire, the Asylum, or Chanonry House, which had a team for former as well as current pupils.

The development of football—which meant rugby—followed much the same pattern, though there were at first fewer local opponents as the

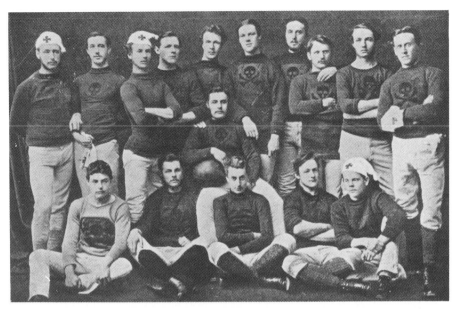

9 'Aberdeen University Arts Football Club, 1872–73'. Back row (left to right) G Cruden, J G Hall, W Gripper, C F Newcombe, J Troup(?), P H Benson, R A Gray, J F Innes, R Wharry, A McG Rose; centre, C C L Skinner; front row, F B Pullin, C L Swaine, D Wardrop, F Newcombe, W B Fergusson. *AM*, 28 (21 December 1910), p. 135.

game spread slowly outside student circles. References to it go back to 1863, and when Ramsay arrived in 1867 he found separate arts and medical football clubs flourishing; in that year they first formed a university team to play St Andrews, at Dundee. In 1870, according to a surviving memorandum book, the Arts Football Club had 57 members, captained by Ramsay. At this stage most of the games were internal ones, including Arts *v.* Medical, Scotch *v.* English (also a popular cricket fixture), and 'Late Gymnasium Scholars *v.* Non Gymnasium'. For outside fixtures, a joint side was formed; a team of present and past players from the Gymnasium provided the only opposition in Aberdeen, but players travelled in 1870–1 to Montrose to play St Andrews University, and in 1871–2 to Dundee to play 'Allcomers', and to Broughty Ferry to play the Dalhousie club. At this time the rugby code was not finalised, many games being played by sides of twenty, but rugby soon became and remained the chief university sport. In 1872 the arts and medical clubs merged to form the Aberdeen University Football Club, but by the 1880s there were again King's and Marischal clubs alongside the University Club, until in 1886 they combined as a single club with three active XVs.[29] There were regular inter-university matches, but a number of city clubs had now developed, and provided most of the fixtures; as with cricket, these clubs tended to scoop up the best players, a practice which, as *Alma* remarked in 1887, 'does not promote the *esprit de corps* which is, or ought to be, an essential feature in all students' bodies'.[30] Without a university ground, players had to use the Links, a large public open space accessible to both King's and Marischal. But no pitches were laid out there, and teams kept their 'poles and touch flags' in the garden of a sympathetic householder.[31]

One of the pioneer footballers of 1870 was George Cruden, who later, as a city lawyer, was the guiding spirit of the Aberdeen Gymnastic Club. In the 1870s its gymnasium attracted many students, especially English medicals, and it seems to have been active socially as well, putting on dramatic entertainments and 'assaults-at-arms'—gymnastic displays with songs and music.[32] Later it became the Gymnastic and Rowing Club, and was one of several clubs which rowed on the Dee, with an annual regatta as the high point of the season. There was a University Boat Club as early as 1870, founded by English medical students. But as was common in the history of sports clubs, it seems to have lapsed for some years, and the annual meeting of the Boat Club in 1884 was said to be the third. By 1885 it had four boats and a 'good shed', and it flourished for many years.[33] Another club with fluctuating fortunes was the Golf Club, which was founded in 1877 and presented with a cup by Lord Rosebery when rector, but later lapsed. It was revived in 1889, and was unusual in bringing together professors and students. A Swimming Club also appeared in the 1880s, using public baths; its activities included 'aquatic football' or water polo, and an annual gala in the summer. 'There were any number of girls there—not a particularly nice entertainment for girls', remarked the prudish Bulloch in 1891.[34]

In the 1870s and 1880s athletics was a popular spectator sport, and at Edinburgh and Glasgow attracted large crowds. In 1873 Aberdeen had a university Athletic Club, which sent two competitors to the Inter-University Games at St Andrews. This event lasted for only a few years, partly because the invasion of professionalism caused unease: in 1873 one of the two Aberdeen athletes was disqualified on the grounds that, though a bona fide student, 'he had one time or another taken part in public and professional competitions'.[35] At Aberdeen there seem to have been no field athletics in the 1880s, chiefly because there was no field. It was one of the university's 'desiderata', and in 1883 the Debating Society passed a resolution, moved by Leask, which called for the building of a societies' meeting-hall and a university gymnasium (something which Glasgow already had). A mass meeting of students endorsed the gymnasium plan, and set up a committee which was also charged with raising £2,000 for the purchase of playing-fields. In 1885 £670 came from a two-day 'Grand

Bazaar' in the Music Hall. These bazaars were a feature of the period, used in other universities to pay for building student unions, and they were organised on a lavish scale: in 1885 there was a long list of aristocratic patrons, stalls were run by county ladies as well as professors' wives, and the raffle prizes included a grand piano and two ponies.[36] But the athletic committee, which remained outside SRC control, was slow to produce results, and it was not until 1889 that the new ground was laid out in university-owned fields behind King's. This was considered 'one of the finest athletic grounds in the kingdom'; there was as yet no pavilion, but there were two cinder and two grass tennis courts, as well as a terrace and a bandstand in anticipation of paying spectators. The ground opened in November 1889 with a rugby match between Aberdeen and Glasgow: Lord Aberdeen kicked off, but Glasgow won 14–0.[37]

The funds had not permitted outright purchase, and the ground remained university property. The university was thus drawn into student activities for the first time, but tried to keep them at arm's length. The ground was leased to a student-run Athletic Association, on lines already familiar at Glasgow and Edinburgh, which organised field athletics, acted as the guardian of the amateur spirit, awarded blues, and represented student interests to the authorities. Clubs for individual sports were affiliated to the Association, which collected an extra subscription for the upkeep of the ground. Complaints about men playing for outside clubs, especially out of pique at not being selected for the first team, remained frequent, and had more justification now that the ground was open. In 1892 Ashley Mackintosh, a keen sportsman as well as president of the SRC, 'condemned, in the strongest terms, those students who join clubs and societies other than those of the University, and recommended that such men should be boycotted by their fellow students'.[38]

The opening of the ground certainly gave games a new impulse. A revived Shinty Club and an Association Football Club both appeared in 1889, though the former had no outside opponents closer than Inverness. In Association football, there were already many clubs in the city—Aberdeen, Britannia, Crescent, Orion, Caledonian, and Ashley were played in the first year—and there was the usual problem of attracting student players away from them.[39] In summer 1890 a tennis club was formed (or revived, for one was mentioned in 1887), and a permanent University Cricket Club combined the three clubs then existing—King's, Marischal, and 'English Students', though the English at first proved recalcitrant.[40] Annual athletic sports were also inaugurated which in the early years, to attract paying customers, were open to all comers and included cycle races.[41]

Alma Mater claimed that the 'socialising effects' of the new sports field would promote 'that brotherhood which should characterise a University more than any other institution', and that nothing tending:

> to lessen the narrow selfishness, to break the unsociable ways of northern academic life has loomed on the University with a heartier reception than the long expected Recreation Grounds. It is to the playground more than to anything else that we must at present look for the fostering of that *bonhomie*, which has been so conspicuous by its absence in our midst.

It also noticed, when the field opened, that 'the energy formerly spent in class fights, is now spent in football', for as in English public schools, sport had the virtue of diverting student boisterousness into more disciplined and socially acceptable forms.[42] By 1891 the magazine estimated that about 100 students indulged in sport, and in 1894 the Athletic Association had 180 members.[43] Sport remained a minority interest, and the popularity of particular sports was to vary; but the structure of men's athletics had now taken on the form it was to keep for many years. One symptom of its new status in everyday life was the appearance of specialist sports retailers advertising in *Alma*; another was its impact on fashion-following students. In summer, 'the most crowded streets of the city are paraded by our friends in the airiest of flannels, with a tennis racquet, carelessly dangled, thrown into the bargain'.[44]

An activity closely akin to athletics was military Volunteering, which attracted the same type of student. The Volunteer movement went back to a French war-scare in 1859, and had become an important Victorian social institution. Individual students had always joined, but in 1885 a special student unit was formed, the 'Battery', attached to the local Volunteer artillery. Medical students took the initiative, and medical professors acted as officers. There were also moves to set up a separate medical unit, and this came into being in 1888, being known successively as the Bearer Company, the Ambulance Corps, and the Medical Staff Corps. In January 1889 the Battery had 82 members, and the Ambulance Corps about 70. For some medical students with army careers in mind, Volunteering had a serious military purpose. But very few Aberdeen students became regular officers, and the main attraction was social. Comradeship was built up through regular drills, church parades, shooting competitions, and local manoeuvres; the high point of the year was the annual camp, shared with other Volunteer units. In summer 1889, for example, the Battery visited camps at Portlethen near Aberdeen, Barry in Angus, and Shoeburyness in Essex, carrying off prizes in various competitions, while the Ambulance Corps had its first camp at Aldershot.[45] In 1891 the Ambulance Corps held its own bazaar, another two-day affair. The Music Hall was decorated as a fortress, and the bazaar was opened by Lord Huntly and visited by Lillie Langtry, then appearing in *As You Like It* at Her Majesty's Theatre. Despite this attraction, the profit was considered disappointing at £500, but it did allow the Corps to acquire its own orderly room.[46]

The ideology of the student movement was most clearly expressed, at the time and retrospectively, by Bulloch and Leask, though these men had personal idiosyncrasies which may not have been typical. In 1891 Bulloch wrote of 'the growth of the new social feeling in the Scotch Universities ... which makes the name University in the fullest sense ... no longer a courtesy title': living communities were replacing collections of individuals. Another comment in *Alma* hailed:

> a new phase of academic life—the increasing social life in our Universities. . . . It has been a cramped existence, an ugly exhibition of selfish individualism, where the sole desire has been to 'get on,' and where all that is implied in the beautiful phrase, Alma Mater, has been a sheer fiction. Mere text-book knowledge, is not the only way of succeeding in life. The socialising influences of University may carry a man further on the path of success than the brilliant display of text-bookism.[47]

This attack on 'individualism' was a constant theme of Leask, who remembered his own student year (1873) as a particularly unsocial one, and involved himself in student affairs in the 1880s as an assistant. Leask thought the intellectual education of the university barren, and criticised what many saw as the essence of the Aberdeen tradition—the atmosphere of competition, hard work and ambition. For him, the 'Smith legend' of the two brothers from Keig had a malign influence, encouraging students to wreck their health by overwork and to neglect true culture. The university had become a mere teaching and examining machine, rather than a centre of disinterested scholarship, and the task was to restore it as a community with a higher spiritual and cultural mission.[48] Inspiration could be drawn both from contemporary movements, especially in Germany, and from history. *Alma* often had articles on the history of the university, mostly by P J Anderson, who became university librarian in 1893 and gave a great impulse to the publication of records and sources.[49] Bulloch too liked to stress the continuity of university life, and the mediaeval roots of such institutions as the rectorship and the 'nations', with much talk of Paris, Padua and Bologna. The quatercentenary of King's College in 1895 was a useful occasion for reasserting Aberdeen's place in the European university tradition, and Bulloch was at hand with a short history of the university, though for various reasons the full celebration of this anniversary was put off until 1906.[50]

The new emphasis on tradition and corporate identity inevitably increased the pressure to wear gowns. H J C Grierson argued at the Debating Society in 1883 that 'a gown universally worn would bind the students together, and instil into them a kind of *esprit de corps*'. But in 1885 fewer than a quarter were said to wear it. In 1888, on a motion by Bulloch, the

SRC organised a plebiscite at King's which produced a large majority (258–32) for compulsion. The Senatus duly reissued the appropriate regulation, but it was never fully enforced, and a plan to differentiate the years by the colour of the tassels on their trenchers was rejected.[51] The SRC set an example by wearing gowns on public occasions, with a special model for the president, and in 1893 *Alma* made a new effort by commissioning a well-known Aberdeen artist, Sir George Reid, to design a lithograph of a red-gowned student for the cover of its Christmas number. Expensively colour-printed in Paris, this was so highly thought of that 300 copies were sent to universities throughout the world, with a Latin greeting from the president of the SRC, and it was often reproduced in later years.

Another tradition given a new emphasis was singing. In 1875, a Choral Society was founded to raise musical standards. Its conductor was Herr Meid, a local music teacher, and from 1884 it included an orchestra as well as a choir. The society attracted a large membership, and its annual concerts became important social events, particularly noted for the attendance of students' families and girlfriends. It acquired the nickname of the 'annual howl', and its programmes remained decidedly on the light side, with dances, marches, and choruses rather than serious classical pieces. The first concert in 1875, however, was notable for introducing the mediaeval student song *Gaudeamus*, which was to become the anthem of Aberdeen students.

Here the German model of student life was especially influential. John Stuart Blackie, professor of Greek at Edinburgh, was a germanophile who published a book of student songs in 1869, and *War Songs of the Germans* at the time of the Franco-Prussian War.[52] His influence was reflected in the *Scottish Students' Song Book* of 1891, which originated at St Andrews but was published as a joint enterprise by the four SRCs. It produced a large income and went into many editions, though much of its sale was outside Scotland, and Aberdeen students do not seem to have relied heavily on it. The Aberdeen representative on the song book committee for many years was Bulloch, who had argued in 1888 that communities, like nations, needed songs as 'a sort of lyric crystallisation of their history, their deeds, their everyday life', and that student songs would hasten the growth of corporate life.[53] Of Bulloch's own numerous compositions, the song 'The Sunniest season of life' became a student favourite for a time. In 1892 the SRC persuaded Principal Geddes to write a pseudo-mediaeval anthem in Latin specially for Aberdeen, the 'Canticum in almam matrem Aberdonensem'.[54] But the most popular new song was 'Shon Campbell' by W A Mackenzie, first published in *Alma* in 1894 as an adaptation of Kipling's 'The Story of Uriah', and devoted to the old sentimental theme of the Highland student who dies from overwork.

One occasion for singing such songs was a new and very masculine social format, the smoking concert. The first 'smoker' seems to have been a Burns Supper in 1884 under Leask's chairmanship, and *Alma Mater* Burns Suppers became regular events for a time. Smokers were especially favoured by political and sports clubs and Volunteer units, and were usually less formal than the traditional dinner, with the emphasis on drinking rather than eating, and with impromptu and collective singing rather than a programme of solos.

Singing was also a prominent feature of the 'students' night' at the theatre. This was an innovation borrowed from Edinburgh, and the first students' night at Aberdeen was held in 1888 after Goschen's rectorial address; subsequent ones were organised by the Amusements Committee of the SRC. The new student ideology demanded that, instead of mingling unidentifiably in town life, students should display a corporate identity to the public. There was already a 'students' box' with its regular clientele, but at a students' night the pit and stalls were taken over, and the night began with *Gaudeamus* and a programme of student singing; if the company was sympathetic, student allusions might be worked into the performance. These occasions often became rowdy, making the theatre management reluctant to allow them, but it usually gave way rather than alienate an important section of the theatre's clientele. Aberdeen had one legitimate theatre, Her Majesty's, which like other provincial theatres at this time played host to an ever-changing series of visiting companies. Farces and melodramas, and the pantomime before Christmas, were the most popular fare in the 1880s, though an occasional Shakespearean company provided serious drama. Frank Benson's company seems to have had a special rapport with students, inviting them to dinner with the cast and getting up teams to play cricket. On Sundays, stage-struck students went down to the station to see the visiting companies off.

The stage was yet another passion of Bulloch. Under his influence, *Alma Mater* gave special attention to the theatre, and in 1888 there was an article on 'The stage as a career for University men' by Arthur Dacre, an Aberdeen graduate who had become a well-known actor. In the 1880s Gilbert and Sullivan performances came to Aberdeen; Bulloch gave a paper on Gilbert to the Literary Society in 1888, and wrote the libretto for a 'comedietta' with a Gilbertian plot and Aberdeen references. This was *The Chair*, put on at the Debating Society finale in 1889. The amateur dramatic tradition encouraged by the finale had already spawned a University Dramatic Society in the mid 1880s, and in 1889 this was revived. In 1890 it put on Bulloch's farce, *The Prof*, though Bulloch's taste had now moved on—he had discovered Ibsen, and gave a paper on him to the Literary Society in 1890.[55] The chief enthusiast in the Dramatic Society was J B Recano, a student with artistic tastes who was also responsible for the fancy dress at the 1890 torchlight procession, and for a keepsake book

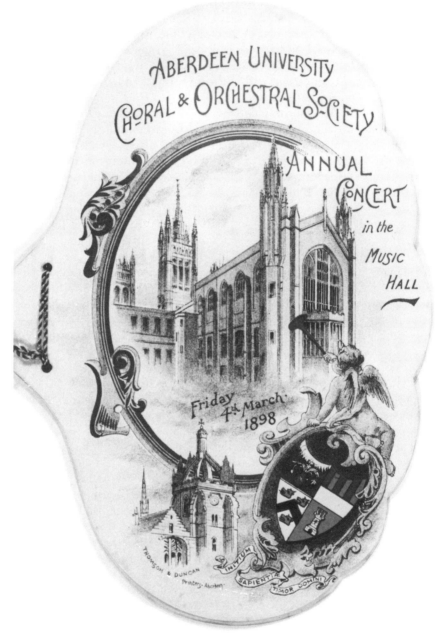

10   Concert programme, 4 March 1898, from a collection in AUL
(Aa, P 83 Cos p).

Programme.

CHORUS, . . "Gaudeamus,"

Students' Song, arr. by Sir H. S Oakeley.

Large Choir

GAUDEAMUS igitur,
Juvenes dum sumus ;
Post jucundam juventutem,
Post molestam senectutem,
. Nos habebit humus.

Vivat Academia,
Vivant Professores,
Vivat membrum quodlibet,
Vivant membra quaelibet
Semper sint in flore !

Vivant omnes virgines,
Faciles, formosæ,
Vivant et mulieres,
Dulces et amabiles
Bonæ, laboriosæ !

Vivat et respublica
Et quae illam regit,
Vivat nostra civitas,
Mæcenatum caritas,
Quæ nos hic protegit !

Pereat tristitia,
Pereant osores,
Pereat diabolus,
Quivis antiburschius,
Atque irrisores !

Specially translated for the Society by
J. Malcolm Bulloch, M.A.

Let us, while in life's fair prime
Join in joy robust !
After youth's delightful time,
After age's cank'ring rime,
Dust returns to dust.

Alma Mater, flourish long !
Mentors, speed ye well !
May her sons, whoe'er the throng,
More and ever more wax strong,
'Mong youth's roses dwell !

Maidens, fair in heart and face,
Joy be ever thine !
Sisters, dowered with charming grace,
Happy—harassed in life's race,
May thy planets shine.

Life to country ! Life to queen !
May our city thrive !
May our patrons' guardian mien,
That protects us all serene,
Long, ah, long, survive !

Woe to harshness, woe to hate !
Woe to fiendish sprite,
Who would dare to militate
'Gainst the student ? ill his fate !
Woe to scoffing wight.

sold at the Ambulance Corps bazaar. The Dramatic Society suffered from having to use men for female parts, and disappeared around 1894. But the Debating Society finale continued, often with farces specially written with local references. In 1894, after a musical first half including 'The Black Owls—a talented troupe of Varsity Minstrels', there was *The Sweet Girl Undergrad*, which like *The Chair* exploited the theme of the female assault on the universities; in 1895 modern dramatic tendencies were satirised in *The First Mrs Cranker-Rae*; in 1897 a woman took a part for the first time—but this proved to be the last finale.[56]

At the other extreme of the spectrum of seriousness, these years also saw a revival of religion, or at least a reorientation of students' interests around the university and its chapel. By the 1880s attendance seems to have been at a low ebb, and in its early days *Alma* ran a series of chapel criticisms, which blamed this on the preaching monopoly of the divinity professors and the quality of their sermons. ('The Rev. Professor's voice and style are as repellent as his religious views.')[57] A few years later, the chapel was restored architecturally and equipped with an organ, and after its reopening in 1891 the services became non-denominational. Distinguished outside preachers were invited, and the Sunday morning services began to attract a large outside congregation as well as more students; the SRC, which encouraged the life of the chapel and attended an annual 'kirking' ceremony, was to complain regularly that students were crowded out of the accommodation reserved for them. Another significant newcomer in the late 1880s was the Christian Association, a university society which took a broad evangelical approach, and attracted a much wider audience than the old denominational and missionary societies. The religious inclinations of students remain difficult to pin down. On the level of church-going and social convention, religion clearly retained an almost universal allegiance. Yet it rarely seems to have aroused passion, or had a marked impact on the university's public life; divinity students (and professors) were regarded by the *Alma Mater* intelligentsia as a dim lot, and their activities were perhaps under-reported as a result. The relatively limited role of religion, once the excitements of Darwinism and the Ethical Society were past, reflected the fairly thorough secularisation of the Scottish educated classes by this time.

One short-lived phenomenon with religious roots was the temperance movement. As editor of *The Academic* in 1877, Leask had called for an extended social life to draw students away from 'evenings spent round the hissing spluttering basins of intemperance'. Leask was a teetotaller, and while his contemporaries enjoyed themselves in the Lemon Tree, he consumed pies and ginger-beer at Johnny Macdonald's pie shop, the only temperance restaurant in the town.[58] Bulloch also criticised the 'bacchanalian individualism' of the old social habits, and was a member of the University Temperance Society founded in 1882, though of its general rather than total abstinence section.[59] This society was strongly supported by medical and divinity professors, and the cause of temperance flourished for a time. Some classes voted to banish drink from their class suppers. The Temperance Society itself held an annual *conversazione*, a format also favoured by religious societies; the term indicated the presence of ladies and the absence of alcoholic stimulants. The society does not seem to have survived beyond 1891, though in 1892 the Debating Society voted in favour of teetotalism, which according to *Alma* 'goes to contradict people who believe that students are merely bipedal beer barrels'.[60] It may be, indeed, that the temperance movement was linked with a shift away from the traditional Scottish drinking customs based on spirits to a student drinking culture based on beer.

Whether the White Cross Union was also a response to real problems is less clear. This began in 1883, and was part of a national 'purity' movement founded in that year, which claimed to protect women by encouraging male chastity; its real target was masturbation, a subject on which it was easy to arouse student guilt. At Edinburgh University the movement claimed 800 adherents,[61] but at Aberdeen the White Cross Army (as it was also called) was said to have 'died a natural death' by the beginning of 1885. It was then relaunched at a public meeting presided over by Lord Aberdeen (a keen supporter of the national movement), with various professors and clergymen on the platform. After most of these had left, Struthers somewhat spoiled the effect with a few bluff words of advice: 'A great deal had been said about natural law; but his advice was to follow natural law as far as possible. If any of his student friends were at all troubled in this matter, let him consult a good medical authority—not a quack doctor—and that was the best he could do'. Other medical professors gave the movement strong backing, but medical students apparently resented the implication that they were less moral than others, and *Alma's* attitude to the White Cross was always derisive; it was last heard of in 1886.[62]

In 1889 *Alma* lamented that students still formed 'separate units', and that the University:

is a stern foster-mother and possesses few attractive and home-like qualities.
The training she provides is fitted to produce able but uncultured scholars—
men full of knowledge, but lacking in social graces and human sympathies.
It is a training rigorous and intellectually healthy, but frigid, socially cramp-
ing, and sadly lacking sweetness and light.[63]

In fact the 1880s had seen the growth of a remarkable range of social
activities, and multiplied the quantity and choice of diversions, formerly
bounded by the weekly meetings of four or five societies, the annual class
supper or grand finale, and the triennial excitements of a rectorial election.
Yet such new activities as athletics, theatre nights and Volunteering, while
helping to shape a sense of student community, were also extending
contact with the middle-class life of the city. The university itself still
provided few social facilities, and once the athletic ground was opened a
student union became the next aim of activists: the SRC set up a committee
for this purpose in 1889, though progress was slow.

The desire to develop 'social graces and human sympathies' reflected
both the need to give students an external polish to conform to new social
standards, and a deeper dissatisfaction with a university ideal which looked
only to intellectual achievement. The growth of new forms of student life
was also connected with the rising age of entry. Older students were better
equipped to run societies, sports clubs or magazines, and to profit from this
training in personal responsibility, committee methods and the handling of
finance. But the age question has another and more complex significance.
Historians have recently stressed that concepts of age and maturity are not
absolute, but historically conditioned, and have argued in particular that
'adolescence' as a separate stage in life was a nineteenth-century invention,
which developed as formal and institutionalised education extended
beyond puberty.[64] This argument seems to have some relevance here. In
the 1860s, Aberdeen students entered at 15 or 16, which was also when
secondary education ended. Middle-class boys who did not go to university (and these were the majority) began to make their living at that
age, and there was nothing odd about treating university students as
adults. In fact their conduct seems a strange mixture of juvenile and adult
behaviour, but with the former (the ragging, noise, and indiscipline)
perhaps outweighed by students' independent life in lodgings, their participation in the ordinary social life of the city, and their relatively mature
interest in politics and university reform.

But as the length of education extended, secondary schools themselves
developed more corporate life, especially through athletics, and a more enclosed and self-sufficient student life built on this foundation. Student-
hood came to be seen, like adolescence, as a separate phase of life, and one
with its own internal development. The stress on the separateness of each

year, from bajans to magistrands, helped students to mature through a graduated series of defined roles, underlined by rituals like gown-tearing and ragging, and by sartorial rules which (unlike the rule on gowns) were rigidly enforced for many years: the most persistent were that bajans were not allowed to wear hats or carry sticks, and that bowler hats were the prerogative of senior medical students.

Looking back in 1906, Bulloch thought that the 'combination on higher lines' which began to replace 'individualism' in the 1880s 'gradually entrenched the student in a little world of his own'.[65] It may seem paradoxical that as the average age of students rose, they tended to retreat into this private world and to postpone their engagement with the adult life of their day, but there were always limits to this process in a non-residential university. In the years down to 1914, as we shall see in the next chapter, the pattern of life laid down in the 1880s developed on the same broad lines. But it had been established under two conditions which were shortly to change: the common arts curriculum, providing ready-made social homogeneity, and the exclusion of women, which had allowed the growth of forms of essentially masculine sociability which were difficult to adapt to a new era.

Chapter 3

Consolidation and Development Down to 1914

In social terms, the most significant result of the Universities (Scotland) Act of 1889 was the admission of women, but there were many other changes, particularly in the arts faculty. The uniform MA curriculum was abandoned and replaced by a system of options, though there were various constraints which ensured that all students still did some classics, philosophy, and science. There was now a separate degree with honours, with specially taught honours classes, which took four years to complete, compared with three for the ordinary MA. The first year of the old curriculum was chopped off, and the junior classes abolished; for the first time there was an entrance examination in arts, and students were expected to reach at school the standard formerly achieved by the end of the first university year. This reflected the rising age of entry since 1860, and the development of effective secondary schools as a result of educational reform in the 1870s and 1880s. These changes, and further modifications made in 1908, destroyed the old homogeneity of the arts class. Although students had similar curricula for the first two years, and a high proportion still passed through classes like English, logic, Latin, and Greek (the position of the classics was sustained for a time by the bursary examination), the range of subjects was now wide, including modern languages, history, economics and political science. The appointment of lecturers to teach them, and to help with the honours classes, diluted the personal impact formerly made by professors. Another innovation was a summer session in arts, devoted mainly to honours classes, and though this was not compulsory a high proportion of students stayed on. This eventually led to a complete revision of the Scottish university calendar, with a three-term year starting in early October and ending in June; this began in 1909–10, though student activities were slow to extend beyond the winter months.

A separate faculty of science and BSc degree were now created. Most BSc courses were in pure science, but from 1895 the university developed courses in agriculture, and later in forestry, and in 1904 the Aberdeen and North of Scotland College of Agriculture was founded to provide practical

11 'The New Poets, or Obliging the Editor'. The student's room in this
cartoon may be compared with that in Plate 2. *AM*, 28 (15 February 1911),
p. 240.

teaching. Other changes following the 1889 Act were the extension of the
medical degree to five years, and an expansion of the law faculty: though
most law students remained part-timers, more subjects were now taught,
and it became possible to take a law degree at Aberdeen. Thus the student
body was more diverse than before, and had fewer educational experiences
in common.

These changes had significant social consequences. The entrance examination tended to eliminate casual or private students, and it now became
normal in arts to follow the full curriculum and graduate. The entry test
might also exclude, as *Alma Mater* noted approvingly, those whose presence 'lowers the general standard of excellence'. For 'year after year, men
pass into the University who, if not totally unfitted for it, would be far
more profitably engaged at a trade, or in cultivating tares and turnips'.[1]
In practice, however, any tendency to social exclusiveness was outweighed
by two new factors. One was the Carnegie endowment, which from 1901
paid the university fees of all Scottish students who applied to it, without

any means test. This supplemented the already generous bursary system. Secondly, new links were established with teacher training. Many Aberdeen graduates had always become schoolteachers, but traditional burgh or parish schools had not demanded any special teaching qualification. As education expanded in the nineteenth century, the huge demand for elementary teachers had been met by separate training colleges. From the 1870s, the Scotch Education Department allowed male students in these colleges to attend selected university courses, though since the college course lasted only two years most were unable to graduate. Aberdeen had two colleges, set up by the Established Church in 1874 and the Free Church in 1875, but these were originally for women only; they were opened to men in 1887, and a handful of 'Queen's Scholars' began to attend university classes. The university also wished to admit teacher-training students independently, and in 1895 this was conceded. These 'Queen's Students' were paid £25 (men) or £20 (women) by the SED, and took selected university courses for two or three years; if they stayed for three, they could graduate. The university created a lectureship in education, and had to arrange practical teacher training. By 1903–4 there were 70 King's Students at Aberdeen (31 men, 39 women), and 41 King's Scholars from the training colleges. But of the latter 29 were men and 12 women, out of total numbers of 41 and 219 respectively in the two colleges: within the teaching profession, university attendance was seen as normal for men, but not yet for women.[2]

In 1906 there was a major reform of teacher training. The state took over the colleges from the churches, and those in Aberdeen were amalgamated to form the 'Training Centre'. King's Students and Scholars aided by the state gave way to 'students in training'. All secondary teachers now had to be honours graduates, and they took their professional training after graduation. Ordinary graduates aiming at elementary teaching could train 'concurrently', in the old style, or after graduation, which became more popular.[3] Though elementary schools were still open to non-graduates, these regulations, which continued in force throughout the remainder of our period, reinforced the link between the university and the teaching profession. They caused an immediate expansion of the arts faculty, which became virtually a vocational school for teachers, especially for women; many science graduates too went into teaching. The arts class records show that teaching was already overtaking the church as the most popular career outlet in the 1880s, and in the class of 1901 40 out of 81 men went into education and only nine into the church, while every one of the 28 women took up teaching. A record of the graduates of all faculties between 1901 and 1925 shows that for the 2,912 men the most popular careers were medicine (1,235), education (777), the church (247) and the civil service (132), but of the 1,627 women 1,101 became teachers, followed a long way behind by 185 doctors.[4]

The editor of the 1901 class record remarked that 'we represent that very sturdy backbone of British life known as the middle middle class, shading away into the eident [diligent] working class, both rural and industrial, with a slight tincture of the upper middle class and even gentry. The core is emphatically the middle class'.[5] Social analysis of students is more difficult in the twentieth century, as the arts class records became less representative once science split off, and eventually ceased to be kept altogether. However, there is a good record for the 1908 class, by which time the admission of women, the Carnegie scheme and the teacher-training changes had had their full effect, and this can be used for comparison with the 1860s. The university remained essentially a local one, and there were fewer arts students from southern Scotland or England (Table 4); but there were notably more students from the Highlands, especially women, reflecting the great improvement of secondary education there. In the North East, the SED's policy of concentrating secondary education meant that few now came direct from small rural schools, but there was a wide network of secondary centres able to give a full university preparation; thus the custom of finishing off in Aberdeen died out. Schools concentrated their senior work on the Leaving Certificate, which corresponded to the university entrance requirement. The Leaving Certificate had a minimum age of 17, and this worked with the Carnegie and teacher-training regulations to impose a more regular age pattern (see Table 5). Carnegie students had to follow standard curricula and show evidence of annual progress, and nearly all the 1908 students, quite unlike those of the 1860s, took the MA degree after the prescribed three or four years.

Comparison of the social origins of students (see Table 7) shows unambiguously that the university in the early twentieth century drew on a wider social range than before. Those coming from the professional and higher commercial classes were fewer, in absolute numbers as well as proportionately. The arts faculty was less attractive to such parents as ministers, doctors or lawyers, perhaps because they were now sending their sons and daughters into the professional faculties without the intervening arts stage, perhaps because wider social and intellectual horizons and greater wealth encouraged them to abandon the local university altogether. The percentage of students coming from farming backgrounds had also declined, as one might expect; a rural background was now more typical of women than men, while men were more likely than women to have been born in Aberdeen itself and to come from the intermediate and working classes. Over half the male students came from these groups, compared with a fifth in the 1860s, and there was a distinct expansion of the occupational range. In the 1860s most working-class students had come from artisan crafts or the countryside, but by 1908 local industries like granite and fishing were also represented, as were unskilled or semi-skilled railway and local government work (see Table 7).

This democratisation reflects the absorption of teacher-training students into the university sector, giving them a fuller education and, in theory at least, a wider choice of career opportunities. The table of origins and destinations (Table 9) shows fewer students going into non-teaching careers, and notably into business; but the existence of a separate science faculty makes direct comparison with the 1860s difficult. In 1901 the university set up an appointments committee to advise on careers, and between 1904 and 1909 *Alma* published a series of career articles later collected in book form.[6] These articles covered postgraduate research, the professions, and various branches of the public service at home and abroad, and they illustrate how weak the links had become with commerce and industry. But it was chiefly the honours minority among the arts students (usually about a quarter at this time) who cultivated these more wide-ranging ambitions.

One result of the changes in the student body was a wider gap between the mass of students and the largely male minority active in student life; teacher-training students, in particular, had little money or leisure to spare. Medical students, with their common curriculum, retained the *esprit de corps* which was fading in arts, and Marischal remained the centre of all social activities, which were more conspicuously than before a preserve of middle-class and socially assured students. There was much overlapping of names between SRC officials, debaters and politicians, and prominent athletes and Volunteers. In 1913 a correspondent complained to *Alma* that 'we find the Societies, the S.R.C., the Sports, though to a lesser degree *Alma Mater* itself, run by a clique composed wholly of Gordon's and Grammar F.P.'s, and almost entirely by those who are natives of Aberdeen', and a university novel set in this period underlined the social gulf between the rural students and the 'sons of advocates' and 'Grammar School youths'.[7] Such cliquishness was by no means new, but it stood out in a larger and more diverse university, and there is much evidence of the social division between country and city students.

The more complex curriculum also meant that students' interests, especially if they were taking honours, began to centre on their academic department. This was reflected in the life of the societies. New ones included the Mathematical Society, the Classical Society, the Philosophical Club, and the Modern Languages Society. The old Literary Society, which was opened to general membership in 1884, tended to become a departmental society for English honours students. Outside the arts faculty, new interests were catered for by the Juridical Society for law students (1888), the Anatomical and Anthropological Society of 1899, which published its own scholarly *Proceedings*,[8] the Women's Medical Society, the

Agricultural Discussion Society, the Theological Society, and the Scientific Association. There was a shift from the self-improving Victorian pattern of debates and essay reading towards programmes of talks by invited speakers, and the younger lecturers and assistants, who came to include some women, did much to keep the societies going and to promote easier social relations among the students.

The admission of women in 1892 was a larger change at Aberdeen than at Edinburgh and Glasgow, where existing university-level courses for women provided the nucleus of a student body. In Aberdeen similar courses had come to an end in 1883–4, and it took time to build up demand.[9] In 1892 and 1893 a few entered the arts faculty as private students—all coming 'from cultured city homes'—but it was not until 1894 that regular students arrived with the full entrance qualification, most bursaries (though not all) being now open to women.[10] In medicine women remained a small minority down to 1914, but in arts their numbers built up significantly after 1900. By 1913–14, indeed, 32 per cent of the university's students were women, and their admission masked a sharp decline in the number of male students in the 1890s, which was stabilised in the 1900s but not reversed; since this affected both medicine and arts, the new entry standards can have been only part of the reason (see Figures 1 and 2).

At first, the 'lady students' (an official term which they much disliked), had a certain curiosity value; their presence inhibited rowdiness in class, leading to a decline of 'passing up' and the rougher forms of ragging and gown-tearing. The women themselves began wearing gowns and trenchers in 1895, and became keener wearers than the men. Female bajans were regularly styled 'bajanellas', though 'semilina' as an adaptation of 'semi' remained humorous. It took perhaps ten years for the admission of women to have its full effect on university life, and while social relations between men and women became easier there was often a *de facto* separation of men's and women's activities. The Literary Society, the Modern Languages Society and the Christian Association welcomed women, who were soon delivering papers and filling official posts. But the Debating Society closed its doors to them, except as spectators, and a separate and active Women's Debating Society was formed in 1897. In the same year two women were elected to the SRC, but this success was not repeated. Although women had the same voting rights as men, there was a feeling that the rough-and-tumble of the heckling meetings was unsuited to women candidates, and that the male majority was unlikely to vote for them in any case. Women candidates stood again unsuccessfully in 1906,

12 'The Gateway, King's College', photograph by G A Clarke. The
students are not named. *AM*, 33 (22 June 1916), facing p. 118.

and this jolted the SRC into creating a separate women's constituency in 1907; its five representatives formed the SRCs women's committee. *Alma Mater* was also slow to open its pages to women. There was a short-lived women's column ('Place aux Dames', starting in 1898), and from 1911 an annual women's number written by women; in 1913 Muriel Mackenzie (later, as Agnes Mure Mackenzie, a well-known nationalist writer and historian) was allowed to edit the summer numbers.

Women thus achieved a limited place in the public life of the university, but this in turn provoked a backlash. *Alma* was often hostile to their claims, and many argued in the 1900s that co-education had proved a failure, and that women should have separate colleges. The presence of women allegedly made men less 'manly', a criticism which reflected unease as the emotional security of all-male social life was disturbed.[11] Others adapted more successfully, and *Alma* began to gossip about affairs and engagements. Reminiscences of the period suggest that there was little unchastity; there may well have been less than in the days of the Victorian double standard, as the presence of women students channelled men's sexual impulses towards the ideal of marriage with a partner of their own class and background. In other universities, halls of residence were built for women to provide the protective and domestic atmosphere which they were thought to need; without such halls, it was claimed, middle-class families would send their daughters to England. But at Aberdeen women preferred to live independently in lodgings, and an attempt to set up a hall in 1898 was a complete failure. This was Castleton House near King's: though sponsored by the principal's wife Lady Geddes, it attracted few students, and lasted only one session.[12]

It had often been argued that the admission of women would have a refining and civilising effect on university life. There was plenty of room for this in the all-male world of student bars, smoking concerts, and class suppers. These activities continued as before, but new forms of mixed socialising did develop—above all, dancing. This was not entirely new, for students had always been able to find partners through their families or friends. A Medical Students' Ball began in 1869, and by the 1880s had turned into the University Ball held every December.[13] This was a formal affair in a large public hall, with an attendance of several hundred, and its committee, though elected by a 'mass meeting' of students, had the reputation of a 'would-be-aristocratic clique'.[14] Following the norms of Victorian custom, 'subscribers' had to submit the names of their lady guests to the committee for social scrutiny. In 1890, for example, subscribers paid a guinea, and were allowed to bring as guests either a lady and gentleman, or two ladies and a chaperone.[15] Professors and their wives attended, but there were also many outsiders, and there was a demand for cheaper and less formal dances which would be purely university occasions. In 1891 the professors' wives took the initiative in organising these dances, to be known as At Homes, or cinderellas (because they ended before midnight). The university ladies insisted on controlling the invitations, and themselves attended to provide chaperonage. The first cinderella was held in February 1891 in the hall of Marischal College; tickets cost only two shillings, and refreshments were 'on temperance principles'.[16] The following year the dances were taken over by the Amusements Committee of the SRC, but for a few years there was friction with the ladies' committee, which tried to control invitations even after the entry of women students. The men eventually established the right to invite their own guests, though women students could not buy tickets themselves; the chaperonage, and the temperance principles, remained. The old Ball disappeared (the last was in January 1896), and down to 1914 two or three 'cinders', with tickets costing only a few shillings, were a regular feature of the social year. By the end of the period, ragtime and other new rhythms were making their appearance; in 1913 there was a 'tango tea' at His Majesty's Theatre where experts demonstrated the new dance—but it was banned at cinderellas. Another sign of the times was the resentment expressed when the authorities locked sitting-out rooms and removed screens which had formerly concealed couples from the chaperone's beady eye.[17]

The At Home—a mixed occasion, usually with dancing—became a common form of entertainment for societies, and in some years supplanted the all-male class suppers, though these did not disappear, and sometimes the women organised all-female ones. By the 1900s, when 'hop' was beginning to replace 'shine' as the slang term for a dance, enthusiasts could dance almost every week. Another form of mixed activity was the picnic, and by the 1900s most classes had a country outing every summer. Like the Volunteer camps, picnics provided welcome relief from the rather rigid conventions which still constrained most social life.

Relations between professors and students were also becoming less formal. If the rituals of the classroom community declined—the Senatus put an end in 1913 to the tradition of Christmas presents—many professors now gave parties at home, at least for their honours students. Principal Pirie's hotel breakfasts were discontinued by his successor Geddes, but principals now entertained senior students or SRC officials at their home, Chanonry Lodge. John Harrower, professor of Greek, looking back in 1914, thought that 'the rise in the age makes it possible to consort with students on an entirely new footing. One is not on the same terms with a man of twenty-three as one is with a boy of sixteen. One has friendly chats in "private hours": one frequently plays golf with him. In my own term of office I have observed an extraordinary change in this respect'.[18] Harrower certainly made a strong impression on students, but usually one of awe rather than friendliness.

Professorial entertaining, like cinderellas, gave a chance for professors' wives and daughters to play a part in university life. But these must often have been stiff occasions; however well-meaning, the high-minded hospitality of the professor's house, like that of the Scottish manse, could be intimidating to the socially inexperienced. Most students were in a 'blue funk' when invited to a professor's 'shine', thought *Alma* in 1895. There was also a sartorial problem:

> The want of a dress suit—that conventional mark of polite society—is often a positive barrier to civilisation. It may seem absurd—but it is a fact—that the man who has not evening dress is ashamed to publish his want by appearing in his 'Sunday clothes.' . . . The dress suit question is at the root of the unresponsiveness of many a man to the calls of Cinderellas and University Balls. There is huge satire in the fact that this state of things exists in a country which next Friday night [Burns night] will be ringing with such proud sentiments as 'A man's a man for a' that'.[19]

At this time, the outfitters Johnston and Laird advertised the 'Alma Mater' Dress Suit for four guineas, or £3. 16s. 0d. with a student's discount. (An ordinary suit cost three guineas, though cheaper ones could be bought elsewhere.) In 1898 they also offered 'The "Professor" Dinner Jacket-Vest', which presumably shared trousers with the dress suit, for 40s. 0d., or 35s. 0d., cash. Dress shirts and other accessories would add to the costs incurred by those whose social life included dances, smokers or theatre nights. For the complete student, Johnston and Laird also stocked the 'Alma Mater' Tobacco Jar, with the university arms—'the latest thing in 'Varsity bric-à-brac, and a very tasteful and useful ornament it is for any man's "digs." . . . Every one with any pretensions to *ton* should have it'.[20] Many students, of course, had no such pretensions. One country student who arrived in 1887 was unable even to join societies or use the university library because he could not afford the subscriptions, and when invited to a party by W M Ramsay he had to make his excuses as he had no suitable clothes.[21] For there were always many students who were too poor, too shy, too prudish, or too pious to join the social whirl.

For the socially active, new attractions appeared in the city in the form of fashionable cafe-restaurants with suites of rooms for meetings and dances. Kennaway's and the West End Cafe were the most popular. In 1897 the women broke new ground by holding an all-female *conversazione* in Kennaway's, with tea, songs and music for 1s. 6d. This 'Lady Students' Shine' was taken as a challenge by the medical students, one of whom infiltrated it in female guise.[22] Women's social occasions became common, and in 1907 the Women's Debating Society held a fancy dress At Home

13   Picnic group at Urie House near Stonehaven, 12 June 1909. *Arts Class 1908–1912: Class Record*, facing p. 91. (Aa P 7 Art 1908–12).

to which men were admitted only if dressed as women.[23] For conservatives like Leask, who had always opposed the entry of women, these social activities were a sign of degeneration and intellectual decay, and in 1912 *Alma* published an outburst in which Leask declared 'that "cinder-men" and "Kennaway women" have devastated the old manly atmosphere by the introduction of the pestilential miasma of a flabby hermaphroditism'.[24]

In fact much socialising continued in separate spheres. While women patronised tea-rooms and the expanding department stores, the male drinking set abandoned the old howffs for fashionable Union Street bars and restaurants, notably 'Watson's' (the Queen's Restaurant), 'Jimmy Hay's' (the bar of the Athenaeum Restaurant), and The Grill.

The theatre continued to be an important diversion, and in 1902 the students' night at *The Belle of New York* was enlivened by a contingent of women who were persuaded to sit in the dress circle in academic costume. 'Their display', reported the SRC,s Amusements Committee, 'was well worth witnessing', and the experiment was repeated.[25] *Alma* continued to give full theatre reports, and in the 1900s sometimes covered the Palace and Tivoli music halls. There were, however, no cinema reviews before 1914. The cinematograph first appeared as a drawing-room entertainment or an adjunct of public lectures. It was pioneered in Aberdeen by Walkers, a firm of booksellers, who both hired and made films. In 1896 they introduced the new invention at a concert which included film of Marischal College and of Lord Huntly (then standing for re-election), and in 1898 their cameraman was active at the medical Volunteers' camp at Stonehaven.[26] It was not until 1912–13 that two commercial cinemas began advertising in *Alma*. The Queen's Cinema offered 'Handsomely appointed Tea and Smoking Rooms. Courtesy. Comfort. Refinement'. But the great days of this medium were in the future.

Students' nights at the theatre still saw a full programme of student singing, a tradition maintained on other social occasions, though it seems to have died out before lectures. The Debating Society finale was held for the last time in the old form in 1897, having been marred for several years by serious rowdyism among the audience. It was replaced by various forms of concert and sing-song, but in the 1900s the Boat Club took up the finale tradition of an annual concert which included a farce or operetta. A Dramatic Society with an interest in serious plays appeared briefly in 1905, and His Majesty's Theatre (re-opened in a new building in 1906) was now offering heavier fare than before. Shaw was presented regularly by visiting companies, and in 1913 there was a visit by the Russian Ballet. In 1910 there was a season of Italian opera, and *Alma*'s reviewer was enthusiastic about *Il Trovatore*, even if 'to our less emotional northern temperament its passionate theme may appear artificial and unnatural'.[27]

If musical tastes were improving, this owed much to C S Terry, who became lecturer in history in 1898 (and professor in 1903). Terry was a noted musical scholar and practical musician, and became conductor of the Choral and Orchestral Society. He attempted to get women admitted, but this was strongly opposed by those attached to the tradition of a male voice choir. Terry had to back down over this in 1899, but got his way in 1904, and was able to train both choir and orchestra more carefully and widen their repertoire. Articles in *Alma* lamented the philistinism of students, but this was itself a sign of widening cultural interests. Students were able to hear W B Yeats at the Literary Society in 1906, and post-impressionism, cubism and futurism were at least familiar enough by 1913 to be the butt of a comic article.[28]

14   Members of Aberdeen University Boat Club in the farce *Chiselling*, 1911. Standing (left to right) C Davidson (stage manager), R W Galloway, K P Mackenzie; sitting, J M Mackenzie, J H Mammen, D Cran. *AM*, 28 (8 February 1911), facing p. 226.

While student-organised social activities expanded, the university dragged its feet over the improvement of accommodation. In 1892, the SRC submitted a detailed plan covering both King's and Marischal, including a gymnasium.[29] The expansion of medical and science teaching already demanded a large-scale rebuilding of Marischal, and it was agreed that this should include a student union. This Marischal extension scheme was controversial, for there was a centralisation party which wanted to abolish teaching at King's altogether and concentrate on a single site. The traditionalists won this battle. The first phase of the rebuilt Marischal was opened in 1895 with a series of ceremonies, though these were marred by student drunkenness and hooliganism, which seem to have reached new levels in the 1890s. H J C Grierson, now professor of English, attempted to define where unacceptable disorder began: 'He was far from objecting to the introduction of applause and pertinent remarks while a ceremony was in progress—that was an ancient privilege of Scottish students—but when catcalls and whistles were brought into requisition, that action passed the confines of traditional license, and became in the highest degree vulgar and ungentlemanly'. Misbehaviour had included 'the intoxication and brutish behaviour of men at the close of the Reception', 'swinish' drowning

15   'Billiard Room, University Union', *University of Aberdeen Quatercentenary Collection 1906*, p. 61 (f. Aa P 13 Qua A).

of Lord Huntly's address and damage to his carriage, and 'howling and singing' at the memorial service for Charles Mitchell, the wealthy Newcastle shipbuilder who provided much of the money for the extension and died just before its opening.[30]

The Mitchell Hall, the chief feature of the extension, was designed for graduations, and also proved ideal for cinderellas; less suitable perhaps were the sitting-out areas in the adjoining natural history museums, where romances had to be conducted before an audience of grinning skulls.[31] Below the hall was the new student union, further funds for which were raised by a bazaar in 1896. It included a debating hall, a dining room, a billiard room, and various ancillary offices, though not the hoped-for gymnasium. Membership of the union was by subscription, and numbers proved disappointing, usually hovering around 200, but sometimes falling below. Membership was almost exclusively medical, and although in principle women were free to join they hardly ever did so. The decoration and amenities left much to be desired—for some years there was no hot water in the washrooms—and since the union was part of a university building it lacked the autonomy of its counterparts elsewhere, and various petty restrictions were imposed. The authorities forbade billiards before 1 p.m. and, more seriously, would not allow the union to apply for a drinks licence, except for serving beer with lunches. Still, students at Marischal could now buy cheap meals—shilling lunches were a speciality—and meet their friends between classes or in the evening. In 1914 the union was extensively refurbished.

At King's facilities remained more basic. The options in the new curriculum gave students spare hours to fill between lectures, though these were still usually over by 1 p.m., so that there was no need to provide meals. Some improvements were made in the old cloak-room or waiting-room, but in 1895 this was replaced by the new sports pavilion, which acted as a social centre for King's during the week. This dual function had disadvantages. There was an upstairs room with a counter serving the traditional jam scones, presided over for many years by Miss Mundie. This had a few benches and chairs, and chess and draughts were provided. But smoking was not allowed, which drove students to use the lower room, normally a changing-room, which offered little but 'sawdust, spittle, and the remains of football jerseys'. Smoking and spitting evidently went together at this time, for *Alma* suggested that if spittoons were provided, as at the union, smoking could be allowed upstairs.[32] In 1908 a new pavilion was opened, and was managed as a common room by the SRC, with a small subscription. Women had their own rooms at both university sites; these were no doubt less sordid than the pavilion, but their minimal comfort is indicated by their nicknames—the Refrigerator at King's, the Coffin at Marischal.

The building of a pavilion marked increasing official interest in sport. The old school of professors tended to regard it as a diversion from serious study, but chairs were now being filled by men who had been student athletes themselves, and had been exposed to the athletic ideal at Oxford or Cambridge, like Harrower, a keen cricketer, or Ramsay, who when lecturing expressed 'his utter contempt of the "molly-coddles" who devote the interval [between classes] to small talk and gossip round the fire, and declared that he liked nothing better than to see his men come in fresh and glowing from exercise in the open air'.[33] Together with the medical professor, Matthew Hay, Ramsay advocated a scheme of medical examination of students, and a levy on the matriculation fee to pay for athletics and other social facilities like the union. The compulsory levy was widely discussed in the Scottish universities, and the Aberdeen Court officially proposed it to the university commissioners in 1894. The SRC at first gave its support, but was later hostile—why should the minority of students who played games be subsidised by the majority who did not?—and the idea was dropped.[34] Instead sport had to rely on voluntary effort, and clubs went through periodic crises. The athletic ground failed to pay its way from subscriptions and gate money, and the Athletic Association fell behind with the rent; eventually the Court resumed direct control, and the ground was managed by a joint 'Field Committee' of professors and students. This was finalised in 1901, and in 1902 another large bazaar raised £810 to put the ground and the Athletic Association on a sound footing. The electrification of the Bridge of Don tramway also helped by making the field easier to reach from the town.

Of the established sports, the one with the greatest struggle to survive was association football, which was harmed by the professionalisation of the game in the 1890s; whether or not professionalisation degraded sport became a hardy annual in the Debating Society. In the 1890s the club lapsed altogether for a time, but was revived in 1898 and came to terms with the new shape of the game. In 1904 it joined the Scottish Football Association, and was regularly knocked out in the early stages of the cup. But university football was vindicated in 1908–10, when C V A MacEchern, a divinity student, played regularly for Aberdeen Football Club, and a student in the 1908 class, George Wilson, was to play professionally for Aberdeen until an injury ended his career.[35] Then and later, it is evident from scattered references that many students spent their Saturday afternoons as spectators at Pittodrie, though this passive role was not approved of by the ideologists of student sport. Association football was never as strong as rugby, whose social cachet gave it a strong position in the local schools. H F Morland Simpson, rector of Aberdeen Grammar School from 1893, an Oundle and Cambridge man, was an enthusiast for rugby and banned soccer. In 1900 it was reported that rugby 'is being taken up by the Gordon's College boys who will form a splendid source of supply to the University teams'.[36] This development, part of a strategy of upward social mobility by Gordon's, meant that Aberdeen had two strong former pupils' teams to provide local fixtures.

Sport at the beginning of the century is described in the report of a Royal Commission on Physical Training published in 1903, reflecting public concern about the physical state of the nation's youth revealed by the Boer War. The chief Aberdeen witness was George Cruden, whose leadership of the Aberdeen Gymnastic Club has already been mentioned. By the 1900s Cruden's Crown Street gymnasium was a centre of student activity, including a university Gymnastic Club. Its staff trained teachers throughout the region, and in 1899 the university appointed Cruden as lecturer in physical training for the Queen's Students. There was still no university gymnasium, but after a petition got up by the SRC in 1899 one was promised in the second phase of the Marischal scheme. It opened in 1907, but there were soon complaints that it was monopolised by the teacher-training students.

Cruden believed in compulsory physical training, and estimated that only about 200 of the 730 students took part in sport. There were 119 members of the Athletic Association, and the numbers in the various clubs were as follows: rugby 50, swimming 50, golf 40, soccer 25, shinty 25, cricket 20, tennis 20, boating 20, and gymnastics 20.[37] A harriers club appeared later, and both men's and women's hockey began in 1903–4; serving teas at the annual athletic sports became an accepted duty of the women's club. Hockey was the only field game taken up by women, and had roots in the local schools. Women also played tennis (this was the only mixed club), and there was later a women's swimming club. Cycling and walking were popular too, but did not give rise to clubs. For both men and women, participation in sport remained a minority taste.

Cruden was a keen Volunteer, and for him as for other witnesses before the commission sport and Volunteering went hand in hand. In the 1890s the Medical Staff Corps was more successful than the Battery, which eventually reached the point of extinction. In 1897 it was replaced by an infantry unit linked to the Volunteer battalion of the local regiment, the Gordon Highlanders. Cruden was commanding officer of this battalion, and Captain W O Duncan commanded the student company. He stressed that it would be 'entirely independent of the professoriate' (hinting at one reason for the failure of the Battery), and it was an immediate success, with about 80 joining.[38] From 1898 the students formed a full company, U Company, and in 1901, to their own satisfaction and that of their female admirers, they were allowed to wear the kilt. All the uniforms and equipment were provided free. There was a daily drill at the Woolmanhill drill hall, and occasional 'march-outs' into the countryside; team competitions in drill and military exercises, gymnastics and rifle-shooting, smokers and dances were all part of the Volunteer scene, the less official side being organised by a Gordon Highlanders Club. The highlights of the year were the summer fortnight at camp, a long and light-hearted account of which became a regular feature of *Alma*, and the annual church parade, when the company marched from Marischal to King's behind its pipe band to hear a patriotic sermon. Cruden told the royal commission that U Company had about 120 students and the medical unit 140, so that Volunteering was more popular than athletics, and attracted over a third of the male students.

Volunteering was popular in all the Scottish universities, as were cadet corps in the leading secondary schools. Should this be taken as evidence of militarism among the Scottish middle class? Student reactions to the Boer War provide some material on this question. South African affairs began to attract attention in the 1890s, and in 1896, after the Kaiser's

16   The Shooting Club Team, 1910–11. Back row (left to right) Pte
J Kirton, Pte J L Smith, Pte D M Marr, Pte J W Innes, Pte A C Macdonald;
middle row, Pte J Morrison, Lance Sgt A Topping, Lance Cpl W G P Hunt;
front row, Pte J M McLaggan, Capt L Mackinnon Jnr (inset), Pte G M Mac-
Gillivray. All members of the team except MacGillivray were in U Company, Gordon Highlanders. *AM, Athletic Album 1910–1911*, pp. xxix, xxxix.

telegram of support to President Kruger, the names of German scholars
and scientists were hissed in lectures.[39] But when the Boer War began in
1899, there was no rush to enlist. It was reported in January 1900 that
'gallant "U" Company has provided several volunteers for active service',
but *Alma* took the view that 'matters have not arrived at such a critical
stage that the Country will look to its future professional men to undertake
duty, which may be performed by others of less fixed occupation'.[40] It
was not a light step to interrupt frugally-financed career plans, and some
of those who did volunteer seem to have been planning to join the army
or go out to South Africa in any case.

The one volunteer who attracted attention was Allan Johnson, a medical
student in his thirties who had been active in the SRC, *Alma*, and the
Medical Staff Corps; he was also the author of *The First Mrs Cranker-Rae*.
Johnson now joined a controversial medical mission which was to work
on the Boer side; in the event it stayed behind the British lines, where
Johnson died of disease. This case seems to have aroused accusations that

Aberdeen students were pro-Boer, which *Alma* indignantly repudiated: 'Let our critics be assured that should ever the necessity arise, the sons of our Alma Mater will acquit themselves in a manner worthy both of British subjects and Scottish gentlemen'. Meanwhile, a joint Volunteer smoker to entertain the London Scottish, who were in Aberdeen for training, was 'quite enough to demonstrate to anyone how thoroughly anti-Boer our University is'.[41] This was also demonstrated by patriotic singing at the graduation ceremony, and by the more serious events of May 1900, when Aberdeen was visited by a pro-Boer speaker, S C Cronwright-Schreiner.

This visit took place just after the relief of Mafeking, when feelings were running high. Students were prominent in the hostile reception given to Cronwright-Schreiner, as they had been elsewhere during his Scottish tour, and the turbulence on the streets in the evening included an attack on the house of Dr Gordon Beveridge, a prominent figure in the labour movement and a town councillor, who had been at the meeting but claimed he was not pro-Boer; as a student in the 1880s, he had been a founder of *Alma* and of the Ethical Society. Next morning the students renewed their attack, besieging the Dispensary where Beveridge was attending patients. They sang patriotic songs, taunted him with cries of 'Kruger', and battered down the door of the room, which the doctors had barricaded. After the arrival of the police the students marched off in procession. In the afternoon they turned their attention to Gustav Hein, the university's lecturer in German, who was alleged to have displayed anti-British cartoons which insulted the Queen. About 200 students at Marischal pelted him with peasemeal and eggs, but he reached his lecture-room in safety. In the evening a large body of students attacked Hein's house, again throwing peasemeal and eggs and breaking windows, alarming his wife and sister. After this the disturbances, which were not confined to students, died down. The Senatus imposed heavy fines on the ringleaders, which were paid by a general collection; it accepted Hein's claim that he had shown the cartoons to his class merely as a teaching aid, but he was also censured for injudicious conduct.[42] The incident certainly showed that political feelings were inflamed, but it fitted into a familiar pattern of non-political rowdyism for which the Johnson affair and recent rectorials (as will be seen below) had given ample practice.

The Boer War made more impact on students than any external event since 1860. The South African adventures of W O Duncan and of various teachers in the medical school kept interest alive. Several students did volunteer for service, and the regular commissions offered to students on special terms by the War Office were taken up. At least one student besides Johnson died. But no lists of war service were published, and there was no demand for a memorial to the dead, though a plaque was erected to Johnson; interest in the war rapidly faded after it had passed its turning-

point in mid–1900. The evidence thus suggests that while no overt opposition to the war appeared among students, and conventional patriotism
was firmly and sometimes violently expressed, military enthusiasm was
kept well under control.

Even U Company, appealing for new members in 1901, stressed that
'it is in no sense the purpose of this Company to recruit for the Army.
The endeavour is to let men get exercise regularly during Winter'; and
Duncan, in a letter from South Africa, commended the Company as 'an
opportunity of meeting with one of the decent sets at King's'.[43] Social
purposes therefore remained to the fore, but the war undoubtedly gave
the Volunteers a boost. In 1904 a unit of student cavalry was formed. This
was an initiative of Lord Tullibardine, commander of the Scottish Horse,
of which the Aberdeen contingent formed two troops. In his proposal,
Tullibardine stressed the value of riding and shooting for those aiming at
colonial careers, though the unit would also be 'a valuable asset, in the
event of invasion'. He wanted serious students, not 'rowdies', the 'object
of the training being to learn to soldier and not to qualify for future
concert singing, &c., though I shall hope to make the time as pleasant as
possible'.[44] Horses were provided free; winter was spent in the riding
school, and in the summer there was a fortnight's training, with much
socialising and sport, at Dunkeld or Blair Atholl, Tullibardine's family
seats.

Despite these aristocratic attractions, the Scottish Horse unit was a
casualty of R B Haldane's military reforms in 1907, which replaced the
Volunteers with the Territorial Force. U Company became part of the
4th (Territorial) battalion of the Gordons, but otherwise continued as
before. Another part of Haldane's reforms was the formation of Officers'
Training Corps in universities, and this was keenly supported by George
Adam Smith, who became principal of the university in 1909, and who
had been a Volunteer in his own student days at Edinburgh. The medical
unit was converted into an OTC in 1912. But Smith's application for an
infantry OTC was turned down by the War Office, and was opposed by
the members of U Company themselves, who preferred their local links
with the Gordons.[45] From the War Office point of view, an OTC was of
limited value at Aberdeen as few of its graduates became regular officers,
while Territorials, unlike members of the OTC, had a legal commitment
to wartime service.

The long non-political rectorship of Huntly discouraged party-political
activity, though current affairs continued to be discussed by the Debating
Society, Celtic Society and Women's Debating Society, and there was a

growing fashion for debates modelled on parliamentary procedure—mock elections or votes of confidence in the government. From 1902 there was an annual Scottish inter-universities debate, and this always took a political form. The opening of the union also stimulated debating, and its debating hall became the home of the Debating Society or 'Debater', as both hall and society were known. A somewhat confused situation arose in the 1900s, with union-organised debates alongside Debating Society ones, and in 1913 the historic society merged with the union, though it was revived after the war.

The 1899 rectorial was uncontested, yet paradoxically proved one of the most turbulent. The new rector was Lord Strathcona, a local boy from Forres who had made good in spectacular fashion as a Canadian railway magnate before retiring to Britain. He was a suitably imperial figure for the mood of the time, and there were hopes that the election of a million-aire might pay dividends for the extension scheme; Strathcona duly obliged, and at his rectorial address in 1900—on 'Imperialism and the unity of the Empire'—he announced a gift of £25,000.

The election campaign coincided with the beginning of the war. The Liberal candidate had been Sir Edward Grey, but he withdrew at the last moment. Grey supported the war, but his backers apparently toyed with the suggestion of nominating Kruger.[46] Eventually no substitute was found, but rather than disappoint those for whom the nomination fight was the main point of the proceedings, events went ahead on the usual pattern. The initial adoption meetings had already been followed by noisy visits to professors' houses, and an attempt to unyoke the horses from a tramcar, accidentally injuring the conductor. The Lord Provost, who had expressed support for Strathcona, had the windows of his house smashed; on the evening before the nomination, paying another visit, students found the house guarded by police. After the nomination and rectorial fight, there was the usual procession down Union Street, and bystanders suffered heavily from peasemeal-throwing. In an attempt by the police to gain control of events, three students were arrested, and when the crowd followed them to headquarters 'the police drew their batons and commenced free play with them'. One student was knocked un-conscious (or so *Alma* indignantly claimed), and a further three were ar-rested. Eventually the six students forfeited their bail by not appearing in court, but the affair was not carried further and no convictions were recorded.[47]

Municipal elections were in progress, and the students' conduct was much criticised at meetings. The police were accused of being unnecessarily indulgent, and the *Evening Express* concluded that 'the licence allowed to the students is being abused, and a widespread feeling has arisen that the only remedy for these outbreaks of rowdyism is to stamp out these street demonstrations altogether'.[48] Some citizens took matters into their own hands, and a band of 'young operative engineers' who had suffered from the barrage of peasemeal decided to break up the torchlight procession held a week later. After leaving Union Street, it was waylaid by some 200 young men with clubs and bags of soot. The police tried to keep the two groups apart, but both they and the students suffered injuries when pelted with wooden pailings, stones and potatoes.[49]

These incidents made the Boer War demonstrations of the following year seem less exceptional. The immediate lesson drawn by *Alma* was that serious political contests should be restored. It deplored the fact that 'the majority of the students, and medical students more particularly, have no political opinions whatever', and called for the formation of political clubs, as at the three other universities, to put this right.[50] The general election of 1900, and the wider feelings of duty and citizenship aroused by the war, eventually stimulated interest. Over 80 attended a meeting to found a Liberal Association in 1900, and a Unionist Association followed. Both made provision for women members. The aged Alexander Bain was a vice-president of the Liberals, but active professors were not involved, for the Senatus, perhaps with memories of the partisanship of the Bain era, had adopted a rule that they should not take sides in student politics.[51] Both associations became permanent, but did not have regular programmes of speakers. Parliamentary elections provoked some party activity, but a more characteristic event was the Liberal smoker in 1901 at which 'pipes were lighted and glasses filled at 7.30, and thereafter a most enjoyable evening was spent'. The toasts included the Unionist Association, a delegation from which was present.[52]

The existence of these associations made the 1902 rectorial, for the first time since 1887, a purely political one, between the Chancellor of the Exchequer, C T Ritchie, and H H Asquith. The campaign stressed national issues—patriotism and Empire on the Unionist side, free trade and the Education Bill on the Liberal. *Alma Mater* commended 'the inestimable benefit of stirring up an interest in political questions amongst the rising generation of professional men—for in another score of years the government of the country will be largely in their hands'.[53] Ritchie won this election, and his installation in 1903 was especially rowdy, including damage to a carriage. Press reports were hostile to the students, after some of the journalists present were 'passed up'. While conceding that this was unwise, *Alma* pointed out that '"passing up" is rather an agreeable sensation . . . the number of hands held out is so great that it resembles lying on a moving spring mattress more than anything else we know'.[54] This led the Senatus to issue such strict regulations for the 1904 graduation—for disorder at this ceremony had survived the transfer to the Mitchell Hall—that students boycotted it.[55] There was further embar-

17 'The Unionist defence after the battle—12 noon—the fight was a draw'. This photograph may be compared with the painting of 1896 (Plate 7). 'Aberdeen University Rectorial Election 1902: the Fight for the Standard', a contemporary photograph album (Aa P 18.3 Ele 1902 f).

rassment in 1904 when a visiting Nigerian prince, the Alake of Abeokuta, was mobbed and had his clothes torn,[56] and the 1905 rectorial saw more town-and-gown friction, a student being convicted by the magistrates for throwing peasemeal at a tram driver; the SRC opened a fund, which raised £65, to finance a successful appeal.[57] The victor in 1905 was Sir Frederick Treves, a distinguished surgeon with no previous Aberdeen connection, put up against Ritchie as a non-political candidate; he and Strathcona (now chancellor) presided over the elaborate ceremonies in 1906 which combined the opening of the final phase of the Marischal extension with celebration of the university's quatercentenary. The SRC's contribution was a new edition of *Life at a Northern University*, edited by Leask and P J Anderson.

A new political development in 1907 was the holding of suffragette meetings in Aberdeen. These attracted women students, one of whom in 1908 appeared on the platform in a gown and moved a vote of thanks, much to the indignation of *Alma Mater*, which normally recommended the wearing of gowns on every conceivable occasion.[58] From early in 1908 the university had its own Woman Suffrage Association, committed to the moderate suffragist position.[59] Its sponsors included a local Liberal MP, but the suffragettes faced a political dilemma in the rectorial election that autumn, between Asquith and Sir Edward Carson. This campaign was run by the two political associations, with lively propaganda on both sides, as well as dances, concerts, and a joint smoker. There was also a union political debate coinciding with the nomination, in which the re-enactment of recent events in the House of Commons, including the ejection of 'Victor Grayson' and of a male 'suffragette', overshadowed any serious political discussion.[60] Asquith was prime minister, and his supporters relied chiefly on the assertion that he was 'the greatest man in the British Empire at the present time'; their campaign magazine was called *The Premier*. But Asquith was also a notorious opponent of women's suffrage; the WSA published a rectorial magazine, *The Suffragette*, which supported Carson, and many women worked for him who were Liberals at heart.[61] Carson got 113 votes from women, against Asquith's 115. Since most women were in the arts faculty, and that faculty as a whole was strongly pro-Asquith, the suffrage factor had a considerable influence on the vote. The figures also show the usual conservatism of medicine:[62]

	Asquith	Carson
Arts	303	197
Medicine	76	116
Science	42	36
Law	8	11
Divinity	6	10
Total	435	370

Asquith's rectorial address in 1910 saw another interruption by a male 'suffragette', and yet another 'carriage affair'. The students were to have drawn his carriage from Marischal to Chanonry Lodge; instead it was smashed up and pushed through the streets into the harbour. There were the usual bills from the hirer, and from the Harbour Board for retrieving the remains, but *Alma* was unrepentant, regarding the episode as innocent fun—'a most enjoyable and indeed witty proceeding. It was typical of student life and student spirit'.[63] It might be thought that the adoption of the motor car would put an end to these incidents, but damage to cars was to be a periodic claim on the SRC's resources in the 1920s.

The two general elections of 1910 helped to keep political interest alive, and there was a rare reference to the student voters who had a university vote because they were MAs (they were worried that the professors might see their ballot papers).[64] But at the next rectorial in 1911 Andrew Carnegie, the great benefactor of the Scottish universities, was elected unopposed. The Conservative and Liberal Associations still existed, but no student socialist organisation had appeared. The labour movement was strong in the city, and there were Labour parliamentary candidates as early as 1892; the candidate then, H H Champion, addressed the Debating Society on tariff reform in 1893, and there were sometimes Labour representatives in political debates. In 1893 the Aberdeen Independent Labour Party claimed students among its members.[65] But there seems to have been little interest, in contrast with Edinburgh and Glasgow, in intellectual socialism of the Fabian type. Socially Aberdeen was one of the most 'democratic' universities in the country, but the rural or artisan background of its poorer students perhaps made it difficult for them to identify with the new working class.

What did appear in the 1900s was a more general interest in social and international questions, coupled with an extension of religious activity. The Christian Association became the Christian Union, and from 1906 the SRC gave official sponsorship to its Sunday evening services in the union. There were also annual weekend conferences; in 1908 the main speaker was the Rev. John Kelman, a popular student preacher at Edinburgh. A new society, the Missionary Settlement for University Women, was concerned with overseas missions, but there was also a university mission performing social work in the Spital, which it was hoped would develop into a permanent university settlement of the kind found elsewhere.[66] Efforts of this kind were encouraged by Principal Smith and his predecessor John Marshall Lang (1900–9), both churchmen noted for their interest in social reform.

Economic, social and labour questions were the province of the Sociological Society, founded in 1909 under the guidance of Stanley Turner, lecturer in economics. In 1912 a Peace Society was formed as an offshoot, and both societies worked closely with the Christian Union. The Peace Society, devoted to disarmament and arbitration and to studying the problem of militarism, owed much to R M MacIver, lecturer in political science (and later a leading sociologist). MacIver had joined the Territorials, but was repelled by the reactionary attitudes of the professional officers he encountered there.[67] Other influential supporters included Andrew Carnegie, who donated £250, Turner's successor R B Forrester, the founder of the Workers' Educational Association in Aberdeen, and D S Cairns, professor of divinity at the Free Church College, who was a vice-president of the London Peace Society with which the Aberdeen group was connected. In 1913 Cairns gave a talk warning of the dangerous state of Anglo-German relations. But the society was more sympathetic to MacIver's optimistic view that social evolution was making war obsolete, and to the argument of Norman Angell, in his book *The Great Illusion*, that the economic destruction caused by modern war would make it impossible to contemplate. A plan to invite Angell to Aberdeen did not come off, but his views were expounded by a visiting speaker at a joint Sociological-Peace-Christian Union meeting in 1912, and in 1913 the Peace Society published one issue of a magazine *Concordia*, devoted to Angellite views.[68]

Edited by the society's student president, W H Sutherland, *Concordia* had contributions or messages from a distinguished array of writers, professors and politicians. But *Alma Mater* made fun of it, and by way of riposte published a special number devoted to U Company and the OTC, with a message from Lord Roberts, the champion of compulsory national service.[69] But one should not exaggerate the political division on this issue. The special military number included a message from Principal Smith, the champion of the OTC, but he was also a patron of the Peace Society, and presided at a meeting addressed by the American pacifist D S Jordan. Conversely, the Sociological Society heard an address from a local leader of the National Service League. Ideas about social reform, militarism and international relations interlocked in a complex way in these years, and student interest in them was growing. Issues like arbitration and conscription often came up in the Debating Society, and in 1911–12 no fewer than three of the debates on its programme were on issues of peace and war—arbitration, war as an instrument of human progress, and whether Britain should increase her armaments. Such questions could arouse a student opinion whose interest in politics was otherwise intermittent, as was also to be true in the 1930s.

Chapter 4

War, Peace and Politics, 1914–1939

The outbreak of the First World War had an immediate impact on all universities, as young men volunteered for service. At Aberdeen, members of U Company had no choice: a hundred of them (half of whom were to be killed within a year) were in camp at Tain when war broke out, and were mobilised immediately without returning to Aberdeen. When the term began, they were already training with the Highland Division at Bedford, where for a time the atmosphere of the peacetime camps was maintained. The soldiers at Bedford read *Alma Mater*, and the magazine had frequent despatches from the Ouse front. In February 1915 the 4th Gordons were sent to France, and an Aberdeen soldier already there reported:

> what could we do but hasten to trace them to their camp and enjoy under new conditions the old familiar fellowship of Quad. and Pav.? . . . They were just the old crowd—the men you sat next to in lecture-room and lab., the men you were sure to meet at Kennaway's or a Cinder., the men who took their share in sport, societies, and S.R.C. They have gone to 'do their bit' for their country just as they used to do it for their 'Alma Mater.' Once their duties were light and there was no peril; now there is a sterner duty and there is likewise a peril, but in that French camp they were still the old cheerful 'Varsity men.[1]

Events soon became grimmer as the unit was involved in heavy fighting in Flanders, and Aberdeen had a black day on 25 September 1915 at Hooge, during the battle of Loos, when D Company of the 4th Gordons (incorporating U Company and a unit from Aberdeen Grammar School) was practically destroyed. At least 15 ex-students were killed in this action—a type of collective experience not undergone by universities with OTCs, whose members were dispersed. Aberdeen's final roll of honour included 341 deaths, out of 2,852 men and women who served.[2] In 1915, serving soldiers left many friends behind, and *Alma Mater* gives a sense of strong emotional involvement in the war, but in later years, with the university denuded of male students, events came to seem more remote, and the dead were already being commemorated in the post-war style, with a list of the fallen read at an annual chapel service by the principal; for Adam Smith this was no formality, for the list came to include his two eldest sons, one of them killed at Hooge.

The effect of the war on student numbers is shown in Table 2. The all-male faculties of law and divinity almost ceased to function, while in arts and science the men left were mostly below military age, getting a year of study to their credit before service. The medical faculty was at first less affected, for while graduates who had been members of the OTC joined the RAMC in large numbers, those still on course were at first encouraged to stay on; in 1915–16 this official encouragement applied only to the final year, and younger students were faced with a difficult dilemma, but before the end of the year it was solved by conscription. The influx of younger students, and the return of invalids, meant that the number of male medical students remained substantial, and the medical OTC remained in being to give them a preliminary training. The most striking medical development, however, was the rise in the number of women students. Before the war there had never been more than 20, until 1913 when there were 31, but by 1917–18 there were 124—many of whom, like the men, seem to have been coming at 16 or 17. They evidently encountered hostility from the men, who resented the fact that their own wartime service was leading to encroachment on their professional preserves.[3]

Between 1916 and 1918 women outnumbered men, and took on the burden of maintaining university life. In the SRC, their representation was raised from eight to 12 in 1916, and it became normal for one of the two vice-presidents to be a woman; in 1920 the constitution was changed so that representation automatically reflected student numbers, though a separate women's constituency was retained. *Alma* also relied more on women, including Isabella Smith, editor in 1917–18, and Nan Shepherd, later a lecturer at the Training Centre and a well-known writer; her novel *The Quarry Wood* (1928) was to have a woman student as heroine. Though slimmed down and appearing fortnightly instead of weekly, *Alma* kept going throughout the war, as did most of the societies. But dances and other forms of entertainment were dropped altogether in 1914, as was men's sport, though women's hockey continued; the athletic field was let out for grazing.

Party politics too were suspended for the duration. In November 1914 Winston Churchill was elected to the rectorship without a contest (F E Smith was to have been his opponent), but never found time to visit Aberdeen. The Peace Society disappeared, and its brand of pacifism does not seem to have led to any anti-war movement; its president, W H Sutherland, won a Military Cross and was killed in action in 1918. Interest in current affairs was kept alive by the Sociological Society and the Christian Union, both of which were very active and continued to propagate a left-of-centre view; the Modern Languages Society was also notable for continuing the impartial treatment of German literature. The Women's Debating Society operated intermittently, and there were occasional debates in the union—conscription being rejected, for example, in 1914.

The general mood, at least as reflected in official sources like *Alma*, was one of sober acceptance of patriotic duties, duties which gave much scope to women. There were fund-raising events for two special causes—a hostel for Belgian refugees in Glasgow, a joint project of the Scottish universities, and the Scottish Women's Hospitals at the front, organised by Dr Elsie Inglis of Edinburgh. In the summer, students worked in factories or on the land. During the term there were organised sewing parties, and the university branch of the Scottish Women's First-Aid Corps, formed in 1913, was pressed into war service. Two enterprises became particularly important: the canteen or Rest Room at the railway station which served meals to soldiers and sailors, and the university Working Party installed at Marischal in 1915, which produced garments for soldiers, hospital comforts, and war dressings. This was organised so that all students could do a stint in their spare time.

After a couple of years, the university settled into a new routine, and there were signs of return to a more normal social atmosphere. In 1916–17 theatre reviews appeared in *Alma*—and one cinema review, of D W Griffith's *Birth of a Nation*. The SRC revived its Amusements Committee, and by February 1917 *Alma* noted that dancing had 'lately spread epidemic-fashion throughout our community', and defended 'the numerous Concerts, At Homes, and Café Chantants which have taken place' against charges of unpatriotism: they were a natural antidote to the monotony of wartime life, and balanced by students' work for wartime charities. A year later, the student organ could report that 'we are recovering from that sense of futility which has been with us from the opening of the 1914–15 session.... this year has seen a general and promising revival in athletics'.[4] Both rugby and soccer teams reappeared in 1917–18, and cricket was played in summer 1918: the ground was still unavailable, but there were calls for the Court to put it in order, and complaints at their tardiness. Another innovation of this session was a Women's Dramatic Society, which put on *A Midsummer Night's Dream*, with an all-female cast, in June 1918.

The war was still in progress when the university re-convened in 1918, but the ground had been laid for rapid revival, and many new students matriculated in summer 1919. This was the beginning of the post-war bulge, as the ex-servicemen who had postponed or suspended their studies returned, with the help of government grants. The medical school cracked at the seams, having double the pre-war numbers in 1919 and 1920, but within four years the ex-servicemen had passed through. As Figure 1 shows, numbers between the wars remained permanently above the pre-war level, but once the bulge was over the overall trend was one of decline. This was due partly to economic depression, partly to changes in the teaching profession which so many Aberdeen graduates entered, and partly to demography, as the birth-rate settled permanently at a lower level than before the war.

But the immediate effect of the war was to increase the demand for secondary education, and the 1918 Education Act marked an expansionist, optimistic mood. Universities were encouraged to increase the supply of teachers, and the new education authorities gave students maintenance grants. In the 1920s the arts faculty prospered and the number of women students rose steadily. But by the end of the decade teaching was over-supplied, and in 1928 the National Committee for the Training of Teachers began to impose limits on training; at first these affected only non-graduates, but in 1932 there was a quota on the admission of graduates to training. These restrictions, graduate unemployment (not confined to teaching, but particularly marked there), and the salary cuts enforced by the government in 1931 as a result of the economic crisis, all made teaching a less attractive profession.[5] The arts faculty began a sharp decline in 1928, and the proportion of women in the university fell from nearly 40 per cent in the 1920s to below 30 per cent a decade later—lower, indeed, than in the last years before 1914. Women did, however, retain a position in the science and medical faculties which they had not had before the war, and these faculties were more buoyant than arts. Science bene-fited from a policy of post-war expansion, especially in engineering, and medicine enjoyed something of a boom in the 1930s (see Figures 1 and 2).

The expansion of arts in the 1920s alarmed many conservatives. Har-rower set the tone in 1918 by lamenting the changes made since 1889, which had destroyed 'broad and sound' culture in favour of 'the strange jumble of subjects . . . that make up the rag-bag of many a student's curriculum'; the utilitarianism of the new students with their minds set narrowly on teaching was particularly deplored.[6] In 1928 the university decided to act. Since 1908 ordinary MA students had had a wide choice of subjects, but in 1914 the regulations had been tightened so that they all had to take a language, a philosophy (logic or moral philosophy), and a science. But the language could be modern, and the science a 'soft' one like geology or zoology. From 1928, however, all ordinary students had to take Latin or Greek, and a 'conjoint course' in mathematics and natural philosophy. This tougher curriculum probably contributed to the arts faculty's decline, and the difficult conjoint course became a standing student grievance.[7]

One interesting innovation was the department of commerce set up in 1919 to award a BCom degree. New lectureships were founded in accounting, banking, economic geography, commercial French and mercantile law. This experiment in business studies (the term was already used) was sponsored by the Chamber of Commerce, and lectures were scheduled at 9 a.m. or in the afternoon to attract part-timers working in offices. The commerce department was reasonably successful at feeding its students into business careers, but in the 1930s numbers fell away (see Table 3).[8] A final inter-war development was the absorption of the United Free Church divinity college, following the reunion of the churches in 1929; the new faculty moved to the Free College in Alford Place, but remained small.

Analysis of the matriculation records of 1924 (see Tables 4, 5 and 10) suggests that the post-war student body resembled that of the 1900s in its relation to the local community and the school system. One important change, however, was that the age of entry, having risen steadily before 1914, now fell back. This is confirmed by figures collected by the University Grants Committee, which show that, especially in the 1920s, the proportion of entrants aged 17 or younger returned to a level unknown since the 1890s (see Table 6). This change, which did not attract contemporary comment, has no obvious explanation. Another statistic collected by the UGC was the proportion of students living at home and in lodgings—which was more or less equal. Women were slightly more likely to live in lodgings than men (being also more likely to come from rural areas), but the percentage of both men and women in lodgings rose in the late 1930s, perhaps because the expanding medical school drew more non-local students.[9]

In the inter-war years, the standard rent for digs was 25s. 0d., though they could be found for slightly less. The cost of living was higher than before the war, and bursaries went less far; in 1937 they were reorganised, 66 open bursaries with an average value of £47 replacing 100 with a value of £32.[10] There were still no halls of residence, despite growing demands for the strengthening of 'corporate life'. It was now that this phrase came into general use; the need to develop the moral and physical side of life as well as the intellectual was part of the post-war mood, and proposals for doing so were often on the agenda of the SRC's Inter-Universities Conference in the 1920s. At Aberdeen, the General Council prepared a special report on systems of residence in 1918, and Leask and P J Anderson put forward a detailed scheme for a hall to be called 'Elphinstone Hall'.[11] The SRC took an interest for a time, but *Alma* expressed a widespread view in doubting 'whether Scottish students have much relish for institutionalism carried into every corner of their lives'. The residential system would check the development of corporate life on current lines and reverse the progress of co-education, and was thus 'not in line with the principles of democracy'.[12] The practical difficulty, as always, was that funds were not available, and that halls were likely to be more expensive than lodgings.

The issue revived in the 1930s, when the UGC was prepared to offer grants for this purpose. When the Committee visited Aberdeen in 1934, the SRC submitted 'that a University Hostel was necessary for the promotion of student spirit and intercourse', and a plebiscite produced a majority in favour.[13] In 1937 the UGC offered £10,000 towards a hall for women costing £40,000, and the issues were debated in the student press. The case for hostels was that 'the sooner students escape from gas-lit, horse-hair-haunted "bed-sits" into well-lit surroundings where it is possible to work in comfort, the better for their mental and physical well-being'. It was impossible to study 'surrounded by aspidistras and moth-eaten antimacassars'. Independence and cheapness were the main arguments on the other side; women at the Training Centre already had experience of the Hilton hostels, opened in 1927, and resented their 10 p.m. curfew and other personal restrictions. Another plebiscite was held, confined to women students, and hostels were decisively rejected.[14] There the matter rested, and Aberdeen was the only British university without a general hall of residence. There was only a small hostel for divinity students in the Spital, started in 1900, and the 'howdie digs' attached to the maternity hospital (howdie is a Scots word for midwife). Medical students had to live in while attending a prescribed number of confinements, though many met this requirement by spending a summer in Dublin. At the end of the 1930s these residential requirements were stepped up, and a hostel was incorporated in the new hospital at Foresterhill, but this did not open until 1941.[15]

The revival of corporate life was especially congenial to the ex-servicemen who dominated the university for a few years after 1919. The best known—at the time as well as in retrospect, for he was an active and ubiquitous figure—was the writer Eric Linklater, one of the many who had sampled the university briefly, in 1916, before leaving for the front. Linklater recalled his student days in his memoirs, and depicted student life in a novel, *White-Maa's Saga* (1929), which well conveys the intensity with which these survivors of the trenches approached both the serious and the frivolous aspects of life.[16] They were men in their twenties, whose social assurance had been reinforced by army life and officer status. The result was a larger gap than ever between the leaders of university society and the mass of ordinary, younger students. Particular tension arose because the women saw their temporary dominance of university life pushed aside by this beer-drinking, pipe-smoking, games-playing masculine boisterousness. The election in 1922 of the SRC's first woman president, Mary Esslemont, was accompanied by a good deal of hostility and bitterness, and was an achievement not repeated, though there were women secretaries in 1932 and 1938.[17]

In the 1920s the 'Varsity spirit' became a catchphrase, and there were constant lamentations at its weakness and calls for its reinforcement. A profile of Linklater in 1922 described him as 'talking Varsity, thinking Varsity, and breathing Varsity,—the true embodiment of that Varsity spirit he has done so much to revive'.[18] Every attempt was made to return to pre-war traditions, including the ban on bajans wearing hats and carrying sticks, though since these items were in any case going out of fashion a new rule against plus-fours was emphasised instead. The gown inevitably returned to favour. *Alma Mater* republished the Reid picture as part of a revival campaign in 1922, and there was some unpleasant ragging of those who refused to cooperate;[19] as before the war, women proved more willing to wear it than men. The anti-gown party argued that 'when we leave the gates of King's we become citizens of Aberdeen in this year of grace 1924, and we ought to dress as such. We ought to do nothing which might serve to separate or to alienate us from the general body of the citizens'. To which a champion of the Varsity spirit replied: 'Let the insignia of the student be stamped upon everyone's back, and *then* there will be no need to cry—"Pull together, Varsity!"'. Such slogans, including the war-cry 'Ygorra' borrowed from Glasgow, were part of the atmosphere of these years.[20]

One obvious stimulus to the Varsity spirit was sport. Most of the pre-war sports were quickly revived, though the boat club was a casualty of war. More emphasis was now put on inter-university rivalry, and a new sporting and social event was the field day, when a variety of teams from

18   'Linkie', a cartoon of Eric Linklater, *AM*, 42 (27 May 1925), facing
p. 344.

one Scottish university descended en masse on another. Sport now also received more official encouragement, and many professors gave keen support. In the medical school in particular, there were ex-athletes like R G McKerron, who attended rugby club dinners wearing his 1889 team cap, Ashley Mackintosh, a great student favourite, or Theodore Shennan, who told the Empire Universities Congress in 1926 that staff support for recreation was essential: 'Over and over again I have got more men to turn out for a contest by speaking to my class and putting the Varsity spirit before them'.[21]

A compulsory athletic levy was enforced by the other Scottish universities in 1929—but not by Aberdeen, where opposition from the non-sporting majority remained strong. However, Aberdeen took the lead in adopting another pre-war proposal, a free weekday afternoon for sport. Wednesday afternoons were conceded in the medical faculty in 1919, and generally in 1922. At first the authorities emphasised that they must really be used for sport and recreation, and much indignation was directed at those who let the side down by skulking in digs or libraries, or patronising cinemas and cafes. In 1923 the SRC resolved that 'individual members of the council should appeal to their constituencies to play the game'. But in 1928 there were still 'too many able-bodied slackers who may be met on Union Street any Wednesday afternoon', who 'can only be termed very poor specimens'. *Alma*'s sports editor reminded them that on the games field 'mind co-ordinates with muscle' and 'you will learn something of the art of dealing with men, and that will be of infinitely greater value to you than the mutual interchange of sexual experiences over cups of lukewarm coffee'.[22] To judge by the tone of the magazine's gossip columns at this time, few of his editorial colleagues would have agreed.

One organisation which made full use of Wednesday afternoons was the Open Air Club, which was formed in 1920 and had sections for walking, rock-climbing, hill-climbing and cycling. Less strenuous outings and picnics enjoyed wide popularity. A love of the outdoors was part of the atmosphere of the age, and non-competitive recreation was more attractive to many than the traditional team games. Summer camps were organised by the Christian Union, and from 1935 there was an annual Scottish universities camp at Carrbridge in the Highlands. In the 1930s hiking and youth hostelling were popular, and there were cycling and mountaineering clubs as well as the Open Air Club.

The ideas on physical training once put forward by Cruden also came into their own, and Aberdeen was the first Scottish university to appoint a Director of Physical Training, Captain A W Brocks, in 1926. In 1927 Mrs Eileen Campbell was appointed as his assistant for women. These instructors made full use of the gymnasium, and organised graded tests and a variety of popular courses, including fencing for both sexes, and

Scottish country dancing for women. Women's athletics received a particular stimulus, and cricket, netball, badminton and lacrosse were added to the traditional hockey, swimming, golf and tennis. In 1938 the university appointed a medical officer and offered a free medical examination to all students on entry; advice was given on physical exercise, though treatment was still referred to family doctors.

A popular feature of these years was the annual athletic number of *Alma*, which included team photographs and records. Introducing the 1927 issue, Brocks stressed sportsmanship and its character-forming virtues: 'Love of outdoor games and play is inherent in the British race, and this love must surely have helped in the formation of the national character . . . It has been said that if you can train a man to be a gentleman to the end of a vigorous and manly game, he will remain a gentleman all his life'. This public-school ideology was something of a novelty at Aberdeen; perhaps a more compelling argument, put in the 1930 athletic number, was that 'from the materialistic point of view the possession of a Blue or Half-Blue may be quite as valuable as a class distinction in securing a good commercial or professional position'.[23]

While the definition of recreation was widened, team games flourished. The old athletic field soon proved inadequate, and the Court was forced to hire various additional grounds, and eventually to open a permanent extension ('New King's', since built over). In the 1920s the Athletic Association usually had 375–400 members, and in 1935 there were 314 men and 55 women—34 and 15 per cent respectively of the total.[24] Estimates of the number of men playing games varied between a quarter and a third, which suggests rather more participation than before the war. When new government grants for recreation became available in 1937, they were used for a new pavilion, incorporating a swimming pool and two squash courts: the courts were only the second in Aberdeen, though a student squash club existed as early as 1935. This architecturally impressive complex was still incomplete when war broke out.

Social life, like sport, soon expanded beyond the pre-war level, though since it took much the same form it need not be treated at great length. Dancing was more popular than ever. For some time after the war, formal dances were still called 'cinders', but the old social restrictions soon disappeared; the new arrangement was for the SRC to be allowed a fixed number of Mitchell Hall dances each year, which it then allocated to clubs and societies. The SRC had to guarantee good order, especially by preventing smoking and the import of drink, for alcohol was not served at the dances. Acting as a steward was a thankless task, and even more so when the Senatus decreed in 1938, after reports of illicit drinking in the men's cloakroom, that a permanent watch should be kept there. Some men also had to be turned away at the door, a problem exacerbated by the new closing hours introduced during the war. Once the pubs closed at nine o'clock, those turfed out were apt to seek entertainment elsewhere, and Linklater, no mean drinker himself, recalled as secretary of the Debating Society in 1920–1 'the necessity of tussling on the stairs with inebriated members of the Third Fifteen'.[25] Rowdyism at debates was a perennial problem, and *Alma* frequently had to denounce the minority of 'sots and hooligans' who spoiled social events for others. 'No dance is considered complete', a correspondent complained in 1931, 'unless there are a few drunk men lurching about the floor, or festooning the sides of the hall'.[26] Besides the Mitchell Hall dances, there were numerous others organised by clubs and societies—there were said to be 80 a year in 1924.[27] New styles of dancing were now fully accepted, and in the 1920s there was a very successful University Jazz Band; a similar Dance Band or 'Rhythm Club' reappeared in 1937, and in 1938 and 1939 there were large fancy-dress balls organised by the newly-founded Overseas Club. Evening dress was no longer required for most dances, though it was for the formal dinners which remained popular in medical, OTC and sporting circles. The old tradition of singing seems also to have been in decay, limited usually to informal sing-songs.

For many students, especially those with more intellectual tastes, the clubs and societies continued to provide a focus for social life. Those which had lapsed during the war soon revived, and new ones were founded. Commerce, Engineering, History, Forestry and Geology were new departmental clubs, and old favourites like the Literary Society continued to enjoy success. The fortunes of political clubs fluctuated (as will be seen later), while on the religious side the Christian Union was reorganised as the Student Christian Movement, representing the non-denominational approach which was always the most popular. This was also expressed in the foundation of a branch of Toc H, and an evangelical bible class became the Christian Students' Fellowship in 1932. Denominational societies were less prominent, though there was an Episcopal club for a time in the 1920s, and a Catholic Students' Society, the first of its kind, appeared in 1939. Generally speaking, clubs seem to have flourished in the 1920s when student numbers were high, languished or vanished in the early 1930s, and revived a few years later. The Choral Society, for example, was revived after the war but later lapsed, and it was not until 1936 that a Musical Society reintroduced orchestral life to the university, followed shortly by a new Choral Society. Another feature of the 1930s was the weekly 'Music Hour' to encourage musical appreciation, run by the university organist.

The first new social amenity was the Women's Union which opened in Skene Terrace in 1925. It included a lounge and dining-room, bedrooms for temporary accommodation, baths and laundry facilities for those living in lodgings, and a large hall used for badminton and dances. There was a subscription of 10s. 6d., but only a minority joined and the union failed to pay; it was forced to close in 1934, and women had to be content with a 'lounge' in Marischal until, after many delays, a new mixed union opened in 1939. This was available to all matriculated students without subscription, and occupied an independent building opposite Marischal, with a proper stage as well as a debating hall; as before, beer was served with meals, but there was no bar. The opening of the union, however, coincided with the transfer of the medical school to the new Royal Infirmary at Foresterhill in the western suburbs, which removed many union habitués, at least during the daytime, and marked the beginning of a drift of academic departments away from the Marischal site which was to intensify after the second war. Meanwhile King's had become a centre of evening activity for the first time with the opening of the Elphinstone Hall in 1931. This provided a new venue for dances and receptions, including the 'bajan binge' to welcome new students.

Away from the campus, the attractions of the town expanded. Much student life continued to centre on Rosemount, and it was an established tradition that whistling a few bars of *Gaudeamus* would draw friends out from their digs for a convivial evening. Chip-shops and soda-fountains, cinemas and cafes multiplied, and some societies now met in cafes rather than university rooms. Two new landmarks were Woolworth's, with its *thés dansants*, and the Palais de Danse in Diamond Street, which became very popular with students and gave them the first real chance to socialise on equal terms, and in respectable surroundings, with their town contemporaries. 'What with the new fields opened by the Palais, and now Woollies,' remarked *Alma* in 1926, 'the Varsity women aren't getting a look in'.[28] The dance-hall and Pavilion theatre at the beach were other additions to the social map.

Alma now regularly reviewed or previewed films, and by the 1930s was covering seven or so cinemas, often with two programmes a week. Cinema-going was probably the most popular of all recreations, and the cinema had the advantage, unlike the theatre, that Aberdeen saw the latest productions at the same time as everywhere else. But in the silent film era the theatre was able to hold its own, and students' nights were revived. In 1921, for example, the performance was preceded by an hour's 'concert supported by student artistes', and in the interval the orchestra played a selection of student songs. The Amusements Committee prescribed 'a minimum of interruption during the acts, with a maximum of corporate hilarity in the intervals'.[29] The diet at His Majesty's was mainly musical

19 A scene from *Antigone*, 1919. *The Book of the 'Antigone'* (Aberdeen, 1919), facing p. 20 (Aa P 95 Ant).

comedies and west end farces, but there were also operatic visits by the Carl Rosa company.

Home-grown theatre too enjoyed a revival. The Women's Dramatic Society followed up its first success with *She Stoops to Conquer* in December 1918, and this encouraged John Harrower to embark on a series of productions of Greek plays: *Antigone* in 1919, followed by *The House of Atreus* (combining two plays by Aeschylus) in 1920, and *Oedipus Tyrannus* in 1922. As a concession to the decadence of the age, these were played in Harrower's translations rather than in Greek, but music, costumes, and choreography were elaborately planned, and women played a prominent part. The plays were long remembered as a success. 'To catch and hold for a steady two hours and a half an audience in the main of Aberdonian bourgeoisie with a leavening of that unreverent animal the student, is no mean achievement', commented *Alma* in 1919.[30] In 1920 the Women's Dramatic Society gave way to a mixed society, and this became an established institution, putting on Barrie, Shaw, Wilde, Chekhov and Synge as well as some lighter events; in 1937 it succeeded in creating a scandal with J B Priestley's *Dangerous Corner*, which was considered sexually daring.

Theatrical traditions were also continued in the biggest post-war innovation, gala week, a series of fund-raising events in aid of local hospitals.
The initiative came from the Royal Infirmary, and was taken up by the
SRC in 1920 as a way of counteracting the image of student frivolity.
Held in April, the gala provided a focus of activity in the previously empty
summer term. Friday, the Aberdeen market day, was the high point of
the week, with a fancy-dress parade in the day and a torchlight procession
at night, both accompanied by collections among the crowds; 'immunity
badges' were issued to shops and vehicles whose owners had made their
contribution. The floats used in the parade could be turned to other uses,
and in 1931 the rector was conveyed on his inaugural visit in 'the S.O.S.
Wrecktoria—a weird-looking "warship" which, under the guise of L.S.D.
Handova, was familiar in the streets of Aberdeen during the students' gala
week. . . . A start was then made with the cruise to the continued shouting
of "Ygorra" by the students'.[31] Painful puns, as well as war-cries, were a
part of the gala tradition.

Gala week soon developed a huge range of activities, and by 1925 the
SRC's Gala Week Committee had spawned 13 sub-committees. There
were house-to-house collections in Aberdeen, and concert parties throughout the towns and villages of the North East; these visits to the 'outlying
districts' became a major operation which exploited students' local links.
Succeeding years saw dances in every possible format, concerts, sports
days, mock trials, collections at theatres, cinemas and football matches,
'beach days' with students dressed as children, swimming galas, carnivals
in parks, a 'motor cycle gymkhana', and 'mounted sports'. Illuminated
tramcars toured the streets, and the Lord Provost allowed himself to be
'kidnapped' for charity. A special issue of *Alma Mater*, later known as the
Gala Rag, combined facetiousness with contributions solicited from well-
known writers, and was sold in large numbers to the long-suffering
citizens. The gala involved students who otherwise enjoyed little social
life—even the shyest or most impecunious could rattle a can—or who
were on the academic periphery: the engineering students always built a
'monster' for the procession, while the agriculturalists set up a shop to sell
donated farm produce; students from the Training Centre, the art school
and Robert Gordon's Technical College were also involved.

The gala incorporated elements from the rectorial ritual and from the
fund-raising bazaars of the Victorian period, and turned them into an
annual routine. It also looked back to the Debating Society finales, for a
musical comedy or a revue based on student life soon became a central
feature of the week. The first was *Stella the Bajanella*, written by Linklater
in 1922, whose theme song became a student favourite. Linklater followed
this with *Rosemount Nights* in 1923 and *The Prince Appears* in 1924. There
were similar shows in 1925 (*One Exciting Night*) and 1926 (*The Witching*

20   Cover of the Gala Rag Magazine, April 1931.

Hour), but from 1927 to 1931 a revue format was adopted with the title *Northern Lights*. The early productions were in halls, but *Northern Lights* soon moved to His Majesty's Theatre, and was able to attract large audiences. It also escaped partly from student hands, being written and produced by a professional team, D S Raitt and William Norrie. The BBC, which had a station in Aberdeen, broadcast excerpts from some of the shows, and the station's director, Moultrie Kelsall, produced *Aurora Borealis* in 1932. In 1933 Raitt devised *Town and Gown*, an entertainment which dramatised incidents in the university's history. This was considered so impressive that it was repeated in autumn 1934 when the British Association visited Aberdeen. There was also a February show in 1934, *The Spice of Life*. Later the gala reverted to musical comedies, mostly written by students under Raitt's direction: *Caravanella* in 1935, *Out for the Count* in 1936, *That's What You Think* in 1937, *Beating Time* in 1938, and *The Varsity Spirit* in 1939.[32]

Once established, gala week regularly raised over £4,000, and there were record takings of £5,577 in 1927. In 1929 there was no gala, because of other appeals to the public's charity, and because the professors felt it was encroaching on students' work. It was revived in 1930, but in subsequent years the event was felt to be flagging—revues and torchlight processions were no longer novelties, and were losing their popular appeal. In 1934 the takings fell to £3,250, and the SRC adopted a policy of '£5,000 or burst': this was achieved only in 1936. But the charities campaign (as it was now also called) was too useful to be dropped.

The atmosphere of the 1920s was in some respects hostile to a serious interest in politics. As editor of *Alma* in 1921–2, Eric Linklater set a tone of unremitting heartiness and frivolity which was to persist throughout the 1920s. There was much fiction and poetry, but few serious articles, and the college columns, following a trend already apparent before the war, concentrated on personal gossip and innuendo. Linklater also set the tone, as secretary and then president, for the post-war Debating Society. This was revived in 1920, and was now mixed. Apart from an annual formal political debate, current affairs were largely ignored and the topics were light-hearted. By 1929 it could be described as 'the only Society which attracts great masses of students drawn from every side of Varsity life, and . . . the only Society whose function has clearly come to be the provision of light amusement'.[33] Only the Scottish inter-university debates, and visits by touring debating teams from America or Canada, provided heavier material.

Conventional party politics revived in the early 1920s, and included a Labour element which lasted until the 1926 general strike, but by 1930 there was an anti-political and anti-party reaction which particularly affected rectorial elections. However, internationalism and the heritage of the war could arouse more passion, and disputes about pacifism and the OTC prepared the way for the more complex politics of the 1930s. The war and its aftermath, including the plight of refugee students, made students more conscious of the outside world. The International Confederation of Students (CIE) was founded in 1919, and Aberdeen belonged to it through the SRCs' Inter-Universities Conference, which had an offshoot called the National Union of Scottish Students for this purpose. (In the 1930s the Scottish SRCs seceded for a time from the CIE, and the Inter-Universities Conference was itself replaced by a new Scottish National Union of Students.) The Aberdeen SRC had an Inter-Universities (later International) Academic Committee which dealt with CIE affairs and arranged student exchanges and cheap travel. On a broader front, the discussion of international questions was encouraged by the Sociological Society, still active in the post-war years but defunct by about 1924; by the Christian Union, run for some years by the future principal T M Taylor; and by the new League of Nations Union (or Society), affiliated to the national body, which inherited the mantle, and some of the funds, of the Peace Society. Progressive ground was thus cultivated on which left-wing politics might grow.

In 1918 Lord Cowdray, a business magnate turned Aberdeenshire landowner, was elected rector without a contest. The first sign of returning political life, in summer 1919, was a Women's Political Association, affiliated to the Women's Suffrage Union, but this did not last. It was only in 1921, with another rectorial in prospect, that political associations appeared: the Liberal Association (with Linklater as secretary), the Unionist Association or University Conservative Party, and the Labour Club, whose president, W E McCulloch, was also president of the Sociological Society. The Labour Club's committee included a student, D Munro, who was elected to the town council in 1921. The club's appeal was couched in high-minded terms, deliberately distanced from the class base of Labour:

> The feeling is gaining ground that the more enlightened, and therefore moderate, element of the Labour Party is the only hope in a dark and stormy time. . . . The time has past when one belonged to a certain party because one's forebears were of that Faith. To-day we must decide for ourselves, and the higher the Ideals held out to us, the more must they appeal to us.[34]

The Labour candidate in the 1921 rectorial was the scientist Frederick Soddy, who had recently moved from Aberdeen to Oxford. He came third, behind the Asquithian Liberal Sir Donald Maclean and the victorious Conservative, Sir Robert Horne, a minister in the Coalition government. The Labour campaign was hampered by lack of supporters, but it was judged that in the peasemeal fight, though heavily outnumbered, 'they put up a remarkably plucky show'. The fight, divided into two rounds, was celebrated by *Alma* as a landmark in the revival of Varsity spirit.[35] The pattern was repeated in 1924, when the victor was Lord Cecil of Chelwood, who had a dual appeal as a Unionist and a champion of the League of Nations; the Liberals put up Lord Meston, an Aberdeen graduate and distinguished Indian civil servant, and Labour C P Trevelyan, president of the board of education in the Labour government. The titles of Conservative rectorial magazines—*Safety First* in 1921 and 1924, *Security* in 1927—reflected the appeal of the party at the time, and there now seems to have been a natural Conservative majority, though rectorial polls were low, and there was little political activity between elections.

The issue of militarism, however, sometimes caused a stir. As early as 1920, a correspondent to *Alma* attacked a chapel sermon by one of the divinity professors as an example of the sanctimonious exploitation of the war by the older generation. He defended conscientious objection, and attacked ministers of Christ who sided with the war-makers, since 'one of the greatest revolutionaries was Jesus Christ. . . . That was the chief reason why the Jewish senatus organised his crucifixion'.[36] Such views may have been quite widely held among ex-servicemen. The head of the real Senatus, Principal Smith, was one of the many clergymen for whom commemoration of the war dead formed a cult in which patriotism and Christianity were inextricably fused. In 1912, and again during the war, he had agitated for the formation of an infantry OTC, and this was now achieved. For a time most students had had enough of soldiering, and even the medical OTC had been suspended, reviving in 1921–2. But the Territorials began actively recruiting student members in 1920, and U Company was briefly reconstituted before being superseded in 1924 by the new OTC. This unit (company sergeant-major: Eric Linklater) rapidly gained a leading position in university life, not least at the Armistice Day service which replaced the pre-war church parade. Principal Smith always visited the OTC's annual camp, and acted for some years as official chaplain, while the commanding officer between 1925 and 1933 was the university secretary, Major Butchart; the Director of Physical Training, Captain Brocks, was also an enthusiast. The OTC thus received the highest official endorsement, and by 1925 there were 163 students in the infantry unit, and 115 in the medical, though these figures fell off slightly in later years.[37] But whereas Volunteering had caused little controversy before the war, the existence of the OTC, and the militarisation of the remembrance ceremony, now caused irritation on the pacifist left.

In 1924 Eric Duthie, vice-president (later president) of the Labour Club, protested against the Mitchell Hall being let to the OTC for a private function, 'when this organisation is not unanimously held to be a desirable feature of University life'.[38] In October 1925 Duthie called on students to sign the 'peace letter' sponsored by the Labour MP Arthur Ponsonby, refusing loyalty to any government which resorted to arms. In the ensuing controversy, which provoked the most extensive correspondence in *Alma* for years, Duthie elaborated his criticisms of the OTC, and attacked the hypocrisy of Armistice Day in the light of the injustices of Versailles and the social problems of post-war Britain. Duthie claimed that his position was supported by ex-servicemen, and it was endorsed by a letter with 22 signatories including various society presidents.[39]

This was part of the background to the general strike in May 1926. It is not surprising, given the mood of the time, that high spirits found a welcome outlet in volunteer strike-breaking—students already had experience of this in the 1919 railway strike.[40] About 300 volunteers took part; students worked at the Donside paper mills and the power station, but were most conspicuous as tram and bus drivers. There were some violent incidents, and the historians of the strike in Aberdeen claim that this left a permanent legacy of bitterness towards students; veterans recalled fifty years later that 'the students were 100% for the ruling class', and that 'they were very different from the student types now—they all came from an upper middle class or what have you'.[41] Sociologically this was not true, though perhaps it was of the activist minority. At any rate, the middle class felt grateful enough, and the 1927 gala saw record takings. The student volunteers were inevitably supported by the university authorities and the SRC, which organised the allocation of work. But Duthie, as president of the Labour Club, issued a leaflet calling on students not to blackleg, though by his own account students did not get involved, as they did at Glasgow and Edinburgh, in the organisation of the strike itself. Duthie's leaflet was not officially authorised by the Labour Club, and this gave the SRC an opening to condemn him. There seems to have been a split within the club, and it did not survive this crisis.[42]

The 1927 rectorial saw another Conservative victory, by Lord Birkenhead (F E Smith), whose propaganda exploited the Labour strike leaflet. The Liberals, still an active force, put up Sir Archibald Sinclair; but there was no Labour candidate, and the third place was taken by John Masefield, the first of a new breed of literary candidates. Birkenhead's speech on anti-communism and the 'glittering prizes' of ambition (a theme first introduced in his rectorial speech at Glasgow) was noisily received, with stink-bombs, fireworks and toilet rolls being thrown, and a cockerel released in the hall. But such scenes were less common than before the war: gala week absorbed surplus energies, and rowdiness was usually confined to university occasions, not inflicted on the town. Rectorial campaigns did have one new feature made possible by the motor car—kidnapping the leaders of rival parties and dumping them in the country-side.

The election of the second Labour government in 1929 helped to revive political interest. *Alma Mater*'s editor that year, Robert Henry, was sympathetic to the government, and an editorial in December 1929 strongly attacked one of Birkenhead's anti-socialist speeches. The SRC condemned this discourtesy towards the rector, forced Henry to resign, and appointed H A Shewan, a pillar of the Unionist Association, OTC, and rugby club.[43] In 1930 the OTC, which now had a weekly page in *Alma*, came under new attack. An anonymous article denounced it as a manifestation of 'the militarist narrowly-nationalist mind which still rules all over Europe', and condemned Smith and Butchart for supporting it. Behind such men, it was alleged, 'stand the grim figures of Famine, Disease, and Death'. In the considerable controversy that ensued, spokesmen for the OTC pointed out temperately, and presciently for 1930, that military strength was a necessity in a Europe where 'there are leaders . . . who are eager and willing to war with anyone. I refer to Hitler in Germany and Mussolini in Italy. These two are undoubtedly a menace to International Peace'.[44] Coinciding with this, a German gun, which had stood as a trophy in front of King's since 1920, was daubed with paint as a symbolic attack on militarism. The SRC had already demanded its removal in 1928, and now renewed the request. But the gun stayed, and the offenders were made to pay for its repainting.[45] A year later, the Debating Society voted for the OTC's abolition.[46] The membership of the OTC showed some decline in 1929–31, but by 1932 it was on the increase, and with its own club rooms and rifle-range at King's opened in 1931, it could claim to be 'Varsity's most popular male society'.[47]

Masefield's rectorial candidacy, sponsored by an 'Independent Association' formed in 1927, reflected a revulsion against the absentee politicians of whom Birkenhead was a typical example. At a debate in 1927, the Independent speaker 'denounced the petty bickerings of party politicians and pleaded that the universities at least be kept free from them. He said that the Independent party stood for a University devoted to culture and not politics'.[48] This movement was found in all the Scottish universities. By the 1930 rectorial the Independents had become the 'Non-Political Party'. Traditionalists argued that without politics the 'spirit and fun of a rectorial would go',[49] but the non-politicals won the day, for their candidate, Sir

Arthur Keith, an Aberdonian medical man and expert on racial theory, was victorious over the Unionist John Buchan, though fewer than half the voters turned out.

In 1931, moving a successful motion criticising the party system of government, a debater 'drew attention to the regeneration of Italy under a dictatorship, and advocated the adoption of a similar system'.[50] Disillusion with party politics, or positive hostility towards them, was a significant phenomenon, for which one may suggest two causes. First, the national decline of Liberalism, which had once had a natural correspondence with the social background and aspirations of Aberdeen students, left a vacuum which Labour, with its quite different sociological base, was unable to fill. Second, the university was now feeling the impact of graduate unemployment, which though rarely discussed in public must have weighed on students' minds, and could be seen as part of a general breakdown of the system. In 1931 a new Socialist Club was founded, but it was also at this point that Scottish nationalism appeared on the student scene. Before 1914, such home rule movements as existed left no trace in the university, whose students in prosperous days were prime beneficiaries of the union. But Scotland was particularly hard-hit by the depression, and nationalism, led by writers and intellectuals, could appeal both as a protest movement and as a dynamic and extra-parliamentary force for renewal.

A Nationalist Association was formed in February 1931, linked with the National Party of Scotland (which merged with the Scottish Party to form the Scottish National Party in 1934). The NPS had itself arisen from Cunninghame Graham's rectorial campaign at Glasgow in 1928, and in 1931 Compton Mackenzie won that post in a famous student victory. The Nationalist Association sought to appeal to all Scots regardless of political allegiance, and made much of its literary links. In 1932 Mackenzie visited Aberdeen to address a meeting, and the speakers lined up for the 1932–3 session included Linklater, Nan Shepherd, Neil Gunn, Moray McLaren, John MacCormick and Wendy Wood. The organisers of the society were two divinity students, Douglas Emslie and William Duff McHardy, who propagated the nationalist cause indefatigably for several years.

Another strand in the politics of these years was a new interest in culture. In the 1920s the terms 'highbrow' and 'lowbrow' came into fashion, and though it would be incorrect to see a sharp division between 'aesthetes' and 'hearties', since figures like Linklater lacked nothing in heartiness, there was a minority which identified commercialised mass culture as the enemy and felt that students were inexcusably philistine. The cinema was the main field of attack. In 1930 an article by 'Diogenes' condemned the films shown in Aberdeen as 'utter tripe'. The *Alma* film critics did not use 'the highly technical vocabulary of expert film-criticism which is not yet crystallized, far less generally known and accepted. We are thus thrown back upon quite inadequate platitudes'. (This was true enough, for the *Alma* reviews were bland and gushing). According to 'Diogenes', cinema must be seen as an art, not mere entertainment, and Soviet work and Hitchcock's *Blackmail* were cited as examples. *Alma* belatedly responded in 1932, printing a serious review of Milestone's *The Front Page*, 'as an experiment, for those students who are intelligently interested in films', and over the next year longer and more discriminating reviews were printed. Critics and correspondents continued to complain of the un-adventurousness of the Aberdeen cinema managers, especially towards foreign films, and the campaign scored a success in 1932 when the Scala showed Pabst's *Kameradschaft* and Clair's *A nous la liberté*. In 1933 the Scala offered Lang's *M*—'a picture to be seen by the discerning. . . . But leave when "*Strip, Strip, Hooray*," comes round'.[51] Evidently the management was hedging its bets; the Scala had a season of French films in 1934, but seems to have disappeared soon afterwards. Aberdeen's flirtation with art cinema was over, and the university cinephiles never seem to have thought of founding their own club. Culture also suffered because the talkies killed off serious theatre; His Majesty's Theatre went bankrupt and closed for a time, and when it re-opened it operated mainly as a cinema.

Cultural elitism, anti-party feeling and Scottish nationalism were ingredients which made the 1933–4 session of particular political interest. In the rectorial election that autumn, there were two political candidates, Walter Elliot, a reform-minded Tory, and C M Grieve (Hugh MacDiarmid), the literary star of the nationalists. But hostility to politics was such that both were put forward in non-party guise. Elliot's supporters, the 'New University Party', claimed to have no connection with the Unionists; they stressed his record as a student leader at Glasgow, his Scottishness, and his war record. His propaganda showed him in uniform, and he was described as 'The Man for the O.T.C.'. Grieve was supposedly the candidate of the 'Students' Party'; he claimed to be strictly non-political, emphasised his youth, and promised to be a working rector who would support the students against the grandmotherly attitudes of the Senatus. The Non-Political Party of 1930 now put forward Aldous Huxley, who was clearly the choice of the highbrows, but there was yet another literary candidate (of the 'Academic Party') in the bulky shape of G K Chesterton. Elliot won, but Chesterton came second, followed by Grieve and Huxley.[52]

In 1933 the SRC decided to revamp *Alma Mater*, which had begun to lose money. Its appearance had hardly changed since its foundation, and its formula now seemed distinctly tired. The editorial committee introduced a new cover and typeface, reduced the price, and declared their intention of stirring up controversy on vital issues; the old jokes and gossip were swept away. Critics complained that 'there has been no light humour of any discription [sic] whatever. This I think is a terrible lack especially in these times of depression'.[53] But the editor argued that humour was part of 'the sunny years' after the war, when the magazine was 'a true mirror of the high spirits of Varsity life'. Today, with unemployment in the teaching and even the medical professions, *Alma* had to reflect realities and encourage rational discussion rather than 'nursery games'.[54]

This it achieved by combining the themes of pacifism, sex, and culture. Pacifism was the deepest strain, and reflected what was perhaps the most fundamental political reaction of these years: the fear of repeating the experience of the trenches and the sacrifice of a generation. The opening article, 'Hate, Headlines and Hitler' attacked newspapers for using anti-Hitler propaganda to stir up war feeling, and further articles argued, from various angles, that opinion was being prepared for a new war through such agencies as the OTC and the armistice celebrations. Even the comic Christmas number, an old *Alma* tradition, worked in some pacifist themes. The impact of this political line was somewhat reduced, it is true, by the continuance of traditional features like sports reports, the Gala Rag, and the OTC page, which carried on imperturbably:

> Drop down any time to the Medical or Infantry Headquarters and have a yarn with the Staff-Sgts. If they can't convince you, try the Presidents of the Union or the Athletic or some other 'heid yin,' and if you are still not impressed let us hope your future calling will be one wherein the qualities of leadership, loyalty, discipline and grit are not required.[55]

Nevertheless, the OTC's publicity acknowledged the strength of pacifism by stressing that military preparation was designed to keep the peace, and was fully compatible with League of Nations ideals.[56]

Tolerance of pacifism had its limits, and they were reached with an article before Armistice Day called 'Lest we remember':

> It is to be expected that we shall be treated to the annual quota of mob hysteria on Saturday, when we are once more reminded of the millions who 'willingly sacrificed' their lives for their King and Country. As we are actually clearing the stage for another war at the moment, it is to be presumed that most of us are unlikely to attend many more such services—not that anyone will worry particularly. So long as we give our elders the opportunity of annual public soul-tearing nobody really cares.[57]

This offended the many alumni who read *Alma*, especially since the losses

21   The Dramatic Society, 1936. Moultrie Kelsall of the BBC talking on 'Scotland in Search of a Drama'. Members present are Isobel Anderson, Sheila Reid, Vivien Strachan, Margaret Barr, Clara Teunon, Betty Scott, Peggy Campbell, Jean Leith-Ross, Lilian M'Intosh, Jack Fiddes, Neil Hendry, Erskine Johnstone, Gordon Wallace, Malcolm Gray, Alexander Cassie. *Gaudie*, 3 (25 November 1936), p. 4.

at Hooge had formed an emotional scene in *Town and Gown* earlier in 1933. The principal now stepped in and threatened to suspend the magazine—a rare departure from the usual policy of non-interference. After some complicated SRC politics, the editor and committee resigned in February 1934, and the magazine did not reappear until June. But the SRC did not disavow its pacifist line, which continued until the end of the year in a more subdued fashion.[58]

Another set of articles dealt with cultural matters, especially the commercialised cinema. 'The England which drove Lawrence from it and still bans *Ulysses* pays millions of pounds to have its instincts pleasurably manipulated, and prostituted, by Hollywood', according to an article which cited *Scrutiny* and Q D Leavis; the author, after a swing at 'the childish barbarism of the O.T.C.', recommended 'the reassertion of spiritual values', and a rather vaguely conceived 'Catholic order'. Another writer, J I W Milne, added to the indictment the popular press, the BBC, an educational system directed 'towards the production of graded and stereotyped mentalities', and the fact that:

homosexuality is not a decently concealed fact but an open and appreciated joke in the majority of our music halls. Where do we, as students, stand in such an age? Let me tell you. We stand in the centre of the mob. We lap up the vulgar journalism, we deal in ideas no less misbegotten and misconceived than these [sic] of the B.B.C.; we are the pustulous adolescents in the reeking picture palaces; we are the stereotyped mentalities; who knows, we may even be the homosexuals.[59]

If so, they were not saying. But this was startling stuff from *Alma Mater*, and the sexual theme was also aired in a review of Havelock Ellis and a particularly controversial article on birth control.

J I W Milne was secretary of the Socialist Club, which was more radical than the former Labour Club. In January 1934 its president, Colin MacIver, contributed an article on 'political consciousness in the universities'. The evils of the capitalist system, he claimed, included 'the creation of a suburban proletariat, dignified by the name of "the professional classes," who are merely the enslaved brain workers of an industrial society'. It was universities who produced this new class, but:

> These cultural institutions have been radically changed in the last fifty years. From being centres of learning leading the existence of a small independent community, they have developed into instruments for the production of young men labelled Masters of Arts, etc., in order to qualify them for certain professions such as teaching, in which they are merely slaves to routine, with only their labour to sell. . . . The pursuit of culture for its own sake is the last thing to be considered in a University career to-day. Such a development, moreover, is an essential feature of a highly industrialized society run on capitalist lines.

But student grievances were now being expressed nationally by the Federation of Student Societies, to which the Socialist Club was affiliated, and which led the fight against war, fascism, and 'all the absurd restrictions imposed on students by reactionary authorities'. The article ended with a stirring call for the FSS to become a mass organisation and act as the revolutionary vanguard.[60]

This critique of university culture was remarkably similar to that of conservative academics. If MacIver identified a 'suburban proletariat', it was H J C Grierson who found 'something melancholy in the plight of the professional man or scientific specialist who has no resources outside his profession or subject beyond golf, bridge, and perhaps the novels of P. G. Wodehouse'.[61] But attacks on the 'stereotyped' curriculum and the 'reactionary' authorities reflected specific student grievances, particularly the mathematical conjoint course. In the 1920s the SRC had taken little interest in curricular questions, but this now changed, and in 1931 it set up a committee on reform of the MA.[62] C M Grieve took this up in his 1933 rectorial campaign, condemning the conjoint course and other arbitrary regulations, and declaring that freedom of choice was the true Scottish tradition.[63] The SRC also felt that its official representations were brushed aside by the Senatus, and resented disciplinary attitudes in matters like the Mitchell Hall dances. When Walter Elliot was elected rector, the SRC asked him to appoint its president as assessor. Elliot managed to divert this demand, pointing out the lack of continuity it would cause, but he persuaded the Court to set up an 'Intermediary Committee' to deal with contentious issues.[64] This did not prevent a 'Students' Progressive Party' contesting the SRC elections in 1935 on a platform of reforming the lecture system, and winning some seats.[65] The new committee met only five times between 1934 and 1939, but in 1939 the SRC's programmes for reforming the MA and BSc were the subjects discussed, and the case against the conjoint course was eventually accepted.[66]

No similar committee was set up for liaison with the Senatus, where the everyday grievances arose, and the SRC decided to take a stand on the issue of ragging. The ragging of medical 'lambs' went back at least to the 1890s, and was later extended to arts bajans, continuing the older tradition of crushing and gown-tearing.[67] Ragging seems to have become a more elaborate ritual after the war: students were 'captured' by their elders, smeared with treacle, soot, soap, paraffin or paint, had their clothes ripped, and were driven in a procession down Union Street before the eyes of the public. It may have been concern for the university's image which made the Senatus ban ragging in 1933 and 1934. But this was considered high-handed, and in 1934 the SRC prepared a symbolic demonstration of defiance. A procession with bands and carnival costumes marched with the captured lambs from Marischal via King's to 'Downie's cairn', where the 'shearing' of the lambs' hair was performed by the president and executive of the SRC. The aim was to show that it was a good-humoured affair which had the full consent of the victims.[68] Nevertheless, the SRC seems to have accepted the ban in later years.

In 1933–4 *Alma* gave a platform to socialism and pacifism, but these were by no means the only political tendencies in the university. For some years, the Debating Society had been in low waters, and successive committees struggled to draw up attractive programmes. In 1934 it was decided to restage the 'King and Country' debate held at Oxford in 1933, and to hold a debate on fascism. At the king and country debate, the pacifist case was put by MacIver and opposed by A R H Kellas, and was lost—an event

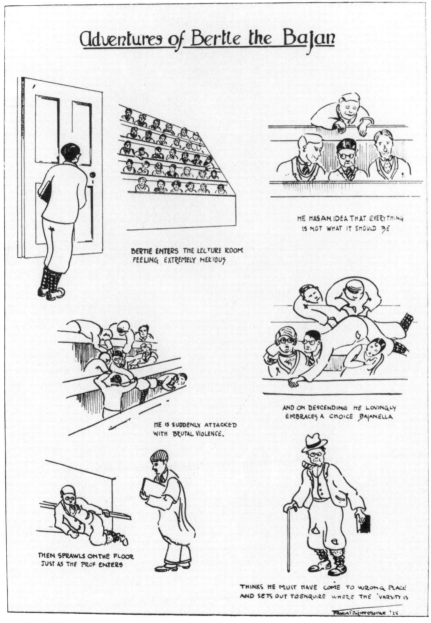

22   'The Adventures of Bertie the Bajan' by M F H Greenhorne, *AM*, 46
(15 November 1928), p. 42.

which did not attract worldwide attention. For the debate on fascism, it was originally hoped to secure James Maxton and Oswald Mosley, but the society settled for Fenner Brockway and William Joyce, the propaganda director of Mosley's British Union of Fascists, then at the height of its influence. The proposition that 'Fascism is the greatest menace to western civilisation' was defeated, as the secretary somewhat naively recorded:

> Mr. Brockway led off with a fighting speech in the good old Left-Wing style—roundly accusing the Fascists of being the tools of big business to grind the faces of the working classes, &c. Mr. Joyce (resplendent in uniform) then got up and delivered a superb speech (from the debating point of view), and turned the tables on Mr. Brockway very neatly. . . . The summing up speeches were as good as the opening, but Mr. Joyce swayed the house by the superficial brilliance of his arguments, so that the negative won by a substantial majority.[69]

Alma also swung to the right. In view of the continuing financial problems, the SRC decided to set up a Publications Committee, under Douglas Emslie, and to launch a weekly news broadsheet, *Gaudie*. This was a success, and was much more lively than the old *Alma*; it modelled itself on the popular press of the day, tried to present news sharply, and was well illustrated. New features included, for a time, a woman's column, 'Pandora's Box', which dealt with fashion, recipes, beauty, personal problems, and the latest arrivals in the Aberdeen shops. In 1934–5 there were 18 issues of *Gaudie* with a circulation of 600 to 700, while the three issues of *Alma* sold between 446 and 600, though the biggest seller of all (750 copies) was the *Athletic Alma* with its team photographs.[70]

Alma was now meant to be a mainly literary magazine, but its first two issues were decidedly political, containing a variety of anti-pacifist articles, including one ('Eyes Front') in defence of the OTC. There was also a vindication by 'Afrikaander' of the racial policies of the South African government, and an article 'In defence of Germany' by Kellas, secretary of the SRC, who had returned from a visit to the country and was impressed by the Nazi regime. The 'Stray thoughts of a reactionary', reversing the enthusiasms of the previous year's *Alma*, linked modern attitudes on marriage and birth control with communist sympathies.[71] In 1935–6 the magazine concentrated on aesthetic and literary matters, showing the same highbrow tendencies as in its left-wing phase, and adopting a daringly contemporary typeface. But one article in 1936, on 'Real democracy and fascist dictatorship', expounded the fascist programme for Britain. The British people were the prisoners of 'high financial powers and great vested industrial interests', and parliament was 'a mere political puppet-show'. Liberalism had destroyed the power of the people to control economic forces. 'It is the task of Fascism to set right this complete dislocation of authority, and restore to the people the reality of self-government in place of the illusion'. This could only be effected by a 'Fascist revolution' which would establish a dictatorship and create the corporate state. The article caused no special comment or protest.[72]

It is easy to see how in more desperate circumstances fascism might have achieved a student following. As an anti-parliamentary force promising vigorous action, it could exploit feelings of disillusion with conventional politics. To those who found, at a time of middle-class unemployment, that a painfully-acquired education was not going to lead to the expected status and security, it might offer both new hope and an outlet for resentment. Its ideology of leadership could appeal to cultural elitists who felt, with Miss Jean Brodie, that there needs must be a leaven in the lump. Yet there is no real evidence of positive support for fascism. It was said that the new *Alma* of 1934–5 was largely written by graduates rather than students,[73] and the 1936 article may reflect the influence of W Chambers-Hunter, who led an active Aberdeen branch of the BUF from 1936 to 1939. Chambers-Hunter came from a local landed family, but had spent much of his life in the colonies; he had lost his right arm in the war, a particular inconvenience for a fascist. His turbulent street meetings were obstructed and broken up by communists, but the historians of this episode do not mention student participation on either side.[74]

In November 1937, when Mosley himself visited Aberdeen, *Gaudie* published an article attacking pacifists for 'playing into the hands of British Imperial Finance', and defending Hitler and Mussolini. Hitler's racial policies were no worse than what went on in the British Empire, especially the massacre of aborigines in Australia. The only immediate reaction to this was an indignant letter from an Australian student defending his country's policies, though a fuller refutation by a socialist was published later.[75] In January 1938 the Debating Society discussed fascism again, with Chambers-Hunter as the leading speaker, but this time 'an overwhelming majority indicated that Fascism is not the creed of Aberdeen University'.[76] By that time, fascism was seen as a threat to European peace rather than a domestic option. But the experience of Aberdeen does not really support the view, expressed in the existing accounts of student politics in the 1930s, that political consciousness was essentially a left-wing affair, and that in the battle against Mosley 'students and workers marched side by side'.[77]

The Socialist Club disappeared around 1935, but a Unionist Association had been revived in 1934, and put forward the Conservative minister Duff

Cooper for the 1936 rectorial. He will, it was said, 'feel fairly sure of the backing of University O.T.C. besides that of the influential and active Unionist Association'.[78] But 'non-political' feeling was still strong. Eric Linklater, though in effect the Nationalist candidate, presented himself as an independent, and two businessmen, Sir Josiah Stamp and Sir Alexander Roger, were also run. The victor was another independent, Admiral Sir Edward Evans, a naval hero and antarctic explorer. With five candidates, the rectorial fight had several heats, and the SRC had to order four hundredweight of peasemeal in quarter-pound bags.[79] Evans proved very popular, and though not a true 'working' rector he visited Aberdeen frequently, arriving adventurously by air, and took an interest in student life, presiding genially at dances and receptions; his rectorial speech on 'Adventure, youth and duty' epitomised his appeal. He was to be re-elected in 1939, after the outbreak of war, when his opponents included Sybil Thorndike, one of two women candidates; Arthur Askey had also been nominated, though he later withdrew—a foreshadowing of the showbiz rectors of the post-war years.

It was international affairs which led to a gradual revival of political consciousness. In 1935 the national Peace Ballot won a large majority in the university, though only a fifth of the students voted.[80] Neither the Abyssinian crisis of 1935 nor the outbreak of the Spanish Civil War in 1936 caused much reaction in the university, but interest in European affairs was kept alive by the International Relations Society, which had succeeded the League of Nations Union, and by a Reform Club founded in 1936 whose president was Colin MacIver's brother Norman (they were the sons of a Stornoway schoolmaster). Norman MacIver was also active in the local branch of International Student Service, which was especially concerned with student refugees. The Reform Club represented pacifist and socialist tendencies, but it was anxious to appeal to a wide progressive front; it worked closely with the International Relations Society, and went in for study circles rather than political agitation. In 1937, however, it decided to hold a collection for the Spanish government: 'Certain members of the club feel very strongly that this university is far too self-centred; and that it would be good to put before the student body some project of wider import than the usual range of Rectorials, Gala Weeks, and other student activities'. This met the hostility of the SRC, which 'condemned any official student efforts to take political sides in the Spanish War', and of *Gaudie*, which ran a correspondence on the affair and was clearly disappointed when all the letters backed the club.[81] But agitation about Spain was not sustained, and in 1938 *Gaudie* took a more favourable view of the Reform Club, which:

with its near-seventy members, is doing much to instil a little political life into the University, but its task is uphill because of the peculiar conditions obtaining here. . . . There is still a suspicion that a progressive point of view in some way prejudices future employers, be they Education Authorities or medical boards or industrialists, against the holder of that view.[82]

The SRC had always avoided appeals to pronounce on political issues, even when these came from other universities. But Norman MacIver was now a member, and the left could sometimes get political measures through. In March 1937, for example, the SRC narrowly agreed to back a Leeds student who had been imprisoned for pacifist activities among the troops, and in 1937 and 1938 it was officially represented at the Aberdeen Women's Peace Demonstration.[83] But in 1939, when the London School of Economics students' union asked the president to sign a letter protesting at British recognition of Franco, this was felt to be a 'test case of the Council's competency to deal with things political', and the proposal was defeated to 'loud applause'.[84] One result of this 'non-political' stance was that the SRC did not resist German propaganda initiatives directed at students. In 1935 it agreed to send a student to Germany at the invitation of the German student organisation, and in 1936 and 1937 a student choir from Berlin visited Aberdeen and was officially entertained. The SRC also agreed, though only after considering the 'racial aspects of the question', to support a Scottish team at the CIE's student games to be held in Vienna in 1939; in April 1939 it was still planning a dance to raise funds when the SNUS decided to withdraw.[85]

In 1933 the cause of peace was a radical one, directed against the university establishment, but later in the 1930s it became less partisan and more respectable, partly because of its connection with Christianity. Religious ideals were still a part of students' inheritance and upbringing, and Christian worship and moral assumptions were part of the everyday framework of university life. The SRC still took a close interest in the chapel, and many who were not otherwise religious went to the services to hear well-known preachers. Thus when a 'Religion and Life' week was launched in 1937 by the SCM it had sponsorship from every official quarter—from Principal William Hamilton Fyfe, who had succeeded Adam Smith in 1935, from Rector Evans ('We sailors . . . would be nothing without religion'),[86] from the main societies, and from the SRC, which turned out in force at the services; *Gaudie* provided full reports, and printed a special prayer each day. Although the OTC was one of the sponsoring bodies, the main outside speaker was to be Canon 'Dick' Sheppard of the Peace Pledge Union; in the event he was replaced by George MacLeod of Govan (later of Iona), whose address on 'Pacifism and Christianity' made a deep impression. The week was repeated in 1938.[87]

The participation of D S Cairns in 'Religion and Life' week was a direct link with the rather similar peace agitation before 1914, with the Reform Club and the International Relations Society (which merged in 1939) replicating the roles of the Sociological and Peace Societies. At the beginning of 1938 a non-partisan Peace Council was founded to bring together all the societies interested in the question. These included the Unionist Association, for the government's policy of appeasement could also be seen as a search for peace. But this consensus did not survive the Munich crisis, which occurred just before the session began in 1938. At a special Peace Council meeting, nearly all the speakers were 'rabidly anti-Chamberlain', and at the Reform Club, 'the secretary received continued heckling for defending the surrender of Czecho-Slovakia in the interests of peace'.[88] The Unionist Association seems to have collapsed, and the secretary of the Debating Society had difficulty finding pro-government speakers for a debate on appeasement. When the debate was held—the first in the new union—a hundred had to be turned away from the hall, and appeasement was rejected by 233 votes to 160. One novelty was the presence of 'a small unit of bona-fide Communists', though these were not students, and no university communist group was ever organised.[89]

The prospect of a war involving Britain stirred student emotions in a way that distant causes like Spain could not, and the Munich crisis was a turning point in reminding them that they were 'the generation that will pay'—the title of a League of Nations Union conference at Dundee in spring 1939. In May 1938, an Aberdeen branch of the University Labour Federation had been formed by MacIver, and the support revealed in the appeasement debate led to the revival of a Labour Club in 1939, though the tone was one of genteel idealism: 'The prime object will be to give progressively minded students something active to do for peace and progress—selling literature, campaigning in elections and at other times, taking part in study-circles, and investigating social problems under expert guidance'.[90] At the 1939 May Day demonstration, the red gown was on display. A Liberal Club appeared at the same time, but the most radical force was Scottish nationalism, now under the influence of Douglas Young, assistant in Greek. Young was a socialist, and led the wing of the SNP which refused to accept conscription when this was introduced in 1939. In April the SRC organised a meeting on the subject, which was supposed to be strictly non-political. But it proved turbulent, since both socialists and nationalists used it to propagate their views. MacIver, following the official line of the Labour party, argued that conscription was unacceptable unless accompanied by a 'conscription of wealth' and the democratisation of the army, but the Nationalist Association opposed it unconditionally. Their president, Donald Begg, used the constitutional argument that only a Scottish parliament had the right to impose conscription on Scots, but also claimed that the government was a fundamentally reactionary one which had no will to fight the dictators, and wanted conscription to control the people and break strikes.[91] These were no doubt minority views, and the crisis also created a flood of recruits for the OTC. But in 1939, unlike 1914, the mood was one of anxiety and dissent rather than unquestioning patriotism, as students came to terms with the fear that the horrors of the Great War might be repeated.

Conclusion

This has been a study of scenes from provincial life, for throughout our period Aberdeen was a university serving and closely reflecting the life of its region. But the relationship was not an unchanging one. In the 1860s and 1870s the tone was still set by the arts faculty, with its traditional links with the church, and the life of the university was interwoven with the rural, religious culture symbolised by the Free manse of Keig. If Aberdeen students were provincial, their province had its own identity and way of life, and they were involved by it in the great religious disputes of the age. But in the late nineteenth century, new forces like the railways and the press were putting an end to regional distinctiveness everywhere in Britain, and a common middle-class culture was emerging, assimilation into which was one aim of those who worked to strengthen the university's corporate life. The new student customs were successful in stamping a common pattern on Aberdeen graduates, whether their work was in Scotland, England or abroad. But since Aberdeen was far from the sources of national culture, students now tended to be provincial in the negative sense of being isolated from contemporary thought and fashion.

The habits and institutions of corporate life took on their definitive form within quite a short period. But the ideological aims of men like Bulloch were never fully achieved. Students failed to show the dignity, decorum and respectability of which they dreamed, and traditional rituals for the release of energy turned into endemic rowdyism and hooliganism. This affected the public image of the student, and there is evidence of considerable town-and-gown friction around 1900, though relations were later repaired through the gala week and its shows.

Esprit de corps was successfully developed through a range of new activities, but was only fully enjoyed by an active minority. The expansion and democratisation of the arts faculty, as teaching became the predominant career aim, meant that many students, though perhaps more in need of socialisation into middle-class habits than their predecessors, lacked the money to participate in the full range of sporting, social and military

116

activities. Moreover, when women were admitted in 1892 they had to accept the priorities already established. Prestige in the student community revolved around such all-male institutions as the Debating Society, the Volunteer units, the rugby club and the student union, and even the SRC and *Alma Mater* were slow to allow effective participation by women. By 1905 women formed a fifth of the student body, but it took war to break down many barriers, and some of the gains made then were lost later. On the other hand, the impact of women on social life was considerable from the start, and was reflected notably in the immense popularity of dancing, reaching its peak in the inter-war years.

By that time, student life was undoubtedly imparting many social and organisational skills, and giving a good training for busy and comfortable middle-class lives, spent between the church, the office, the golf course, the club dinner and the charitable committee. Even the Volunteer and OTC activities proved more useful than might have been expected, since few male graduates between 1900 and 1939 can have escaped service in the armed forces. But university life was probably less effective at challenging the conventional political, moral and cultural views which students brought with them from their homes and schools. An interest in national politics was stirred up only intermittently, and cultural ambitions beyond what the formal curriculum offered were limited. Between the wars, highbrows strove to improve things, but the general taste of students remained relentlessly middlebrow. This was demonstrated by the gala shows of that period, but the theatrical and musical enthusiasms of the nineteenth century, and the style of light magazine journalism adopted by *Alma Mater*, show that little had changed in this respect. Students were seldom well-informed about the contemporary arts, and certainly did not form a creative avant-garde as was sometimes the case with students in other countries.

The cafes of Aberdeen, though popular with students, were not the cafes of Paris, and at no time was a bohemian life style cultivated. Student social customs were modelled on those of the adult world, and in dress and general behaviour students were anxious to follow conventional models. This is perhaps one of the things which has changed most since 1939. For student life in our period had a public, urban aspect which was at that time shared by the wider middle-class community. When students paraded in Union Street, applauded their favourite theatrical companies, or patronised fashionable bars, tea rooms, cinemas and department stores, they were enjoying the same kind of social life as their adult contemporaries. Since then, adult life has become more private and suburban, centred on the family and the home. Temporary exiles from the consumer society, students remain faithful to an older ideal of collective, public enjoyment. In this they share the position of the young and unmarried generally, and as a result the norms of student life relate to a generational rather than a class ideal, expressed culturally in musical and sartorial tastes. Before 1939, by contrast, the lives of students and of working-class youth were worlds apart.

This study has deliberately refrained from pointing out similarities or differences between past and present. It would seem that the patterns of student life described here persisted until at least the 1960s, but that since then there have been global changes in youth culture and generational attitudes. The introduction of a more relaxed life style, with less need for the release of tension, may account for the decay of the traditional demonstrative rowdyism. Certain changes have been specific to Aberdeen. The old ties between the university and the life of the city have been weakened by the retreat of the university from Marischal to King's— a process just beginning at the end of the 1930s—and by the declining importance of the landlady and the large-scale construction of halls of residence. In this move towards residence, Aberdeen has followed the general British trend for students to leave their home communities, and for universities to detach themselves from their local roots. The loosening of the links between university, city and region puts an end to the phase of student life described in this study; whether this is a loss or a gain is for the reader to judge.

Notes

INTRODUCTION, pp. 1 to 5

1   N N Maclean, *Life at a Northern University*, ed. W K Leask (Aberdeen, 1906).
    Maclean also wrote 'University life in the north of Scotland', *Chambers's
    Journal*, 4th series, 9 (1872), 276–80.
2   See R D Anderson, 'In search of the "lad of parts": the mythical history of
    Scottish education', *History Workshop*, 19 (1985), 82–104.
3   W C Smith, *The Poetical Works of Walter C Smith* (London, 1902), 87. The
    poem, 'Borland Hall', dates from 1874.
4   See obituary in *Aberdeen University Review* (hereafter *AUR*), 12 (1924–5),
    231–8.

CHAPTER 1, pp. 6 to 31

1   See Figures 1 and 2 and Table 1. Figures and tables, with explanatory
    comment, will be found in Appendix I.
2   For a more systematic discussion, see D I Mackay, *Geographical Mobility and
    the Brain Drain: a Case Study of Aberdeen University Graduates, 1860–1960*
    (London, 1969) (hereafter Mackay, *Geographical Mobility*), 93–8, 110–15.
3   M Sanderson, *The Universities and British Industry, 1850–1970* (London, 1972),
    178.
4   This percentage is given for each year between 1860 and 1877 in P J Anderson,
    ed., *Records of the Arts Class, 1868–72, University of Aberdeen* (Aberdeen,
    1882), 101. Other details of this kind are in J B Duncan and W Smith, eds,
    Record of the Arts Class 1865–69. University of Aberdeen (Aberdeen, 1913), 73–
    5; A Shewan, ed., *Meminisse Juvat, being the Autobiography of a Class at King's
    College in the Sixties* (Aberdeen, 1905) (hereafter Shewan, *Meminisse Juvat*),
    67; S Ree, ed., *Records of the Arts Class, 1868–72, University of Aberdeen* (2nd
    edn, Aberdeen, 1892), 29; *Aberdeen University Arts Class, 1884–8: Record of
    the Class* (n.p., 1890), 10.
5   Combining data from Tables II (size of first-year classes) and III in *Royal
    Commission on the Universities of Scotland. Returns and Documents* (PP, 1878,
    XXXV), 209, 211. For comparison with other universities, where rates of
    graduation were lower than Aberdeen, see R D Anderson, *Education and
    Opportunity in Victorian Scotland: Schools and Universities* (Oxford, 1983)
    (hereafter Anderson, *Education and Opportunity*), 75. Details of degrees
    awarded are in W Johnston, *Roll of the Graduates of the University of Aberdeen,*

1860–1900 (Aberdeen, 1906), and T Watt, *Roll of the Graduates of the University of Aberdeen, 1901–1925* (Aberdeen, 1935), but not in the continuation by J Mackintosh, *Roll of the Graduates of the University of Aberdeen, 1926–1955* (Aberdeen, 1960). Note that since these *Rolls* include only graduates, they are far from comprehensive.

6   Mackay, *Geographical Mobility*, 74.

7   J Smith and J F Cruickshank, eds, *Records of the Arts Class, 1870–74, University of Aberdeen* (Aberdeen, 1896) (hereafter Smith and Cruickshank, *Arts Class 1870–74*), 14–15. See also R B Strathdee, 'A Scarlet cloke in my land', *AUR*, 43 (1969–70), 245–51.

8   Obituaries in *AUR*, 2 (1914–15), 21–32; A M Williams, *A Bundle of Yarns: Tales and Memories* (London, 1931), 36–41.

9   Smith and Cruickshank, *Arts Class 1870–74*, 17; Shewan, *Meminisse Juvat*, 11.

10 J Demogeot and H Montucci, *De l'Enseignement supérieur en Angleterre et en Ecosse* (Paris, 1870), 503–4 (report on Scotland by Montucci).

11 *Chambers's Journal*, 4th series, 9 (1872), 280.

12 Personal observation.

13 J S Black and G Chrystal, *The Life of William Robertson Smith* (London, 1912) (hereafter Black and Chrystal, *Robertson Smith*), 39–41.

14 *Chambers's Journal*, 4th series, 9 (1872), 279; W R Nicoll, 'The Homes of the rural students, 1866–70', *AUR*, 1 (1913–14), 36–41.

15 *Alma Mater* (hereafter *AM*), 40 (1922–3), 272. See also *AUR*, 24 (1936–7), 116–17, and 25 (1937–8), 45 (the student was Donald Munro).

16 H E B Speight in *AUR*, 40 (1963–4), 265–6.

17 *Lancet*, vol. 2 for 1894, 550; *AM*, 12 (1894–5), 53 and 30 (1912–13), 166; Nicoll in *Alma Mater. Aberdeen University Magazine. Quatercentenary Number, September 1906* (Aberdeen, n.d.) (hereafter *AM Quatercentenary No.*: this number is outside the regular series of *AM*), 38–40; recollections in *AUR*, 3 (1915–16), 119.

18 Details of fees and curricula are in the annual *Calendar*. Those cited are for the 1880s.

19 *Cornhill Magazine*, 1 (1860), 366, 369.

20 Ibid., 375.

21 *AM*, 17 (1899–1900), 94.

22 *AM*, 2 (1884–5), 128; Aberdeen University Library (hereafter AUL), MS 2798/1/2/1, Bulloch diaries, 22 March 1889.

23 See A Keith in *AM Quatercentenary No.*, 42–3.

24 W S Bruce, *Reminiscences of Men and Manners during the Past Seventy Years* (Aberdeen, 1929) (hereafter Bruce, *Reminiscences*), 46; W K Leask, *Interamna Borealis: Being Memories and Portraits from an Old University Town Between the Don and the Dee* (Aberdeen, 1917) (hereafter Leask, *Interamna Borealis*), 321–3.

25 *AM*, 5 (1887–8), 18–19.

26 AUL, MS U 281, Debating Society Minutes, 1860–88.

27 Ibid.; *Aberdeen University Gazette*, 13 February 1874, 75.

28 A M Williams and A Duffus, eds, *Records of the Arts Class, 1876–1880. University of Aberdeen* (Aberdeen, 1907), ix.

29 H Mackenzie, *The Third Statistical Account of Scotland: the City of Aberdeen* (Edinburgh, 1953), 90; see 537 and following for recreation and social life.

30 Leask, *Interamna Borealis*, 64–6, and in *AM*, 17 (1899–1900), 92–4.

31   T C Smout, *A Century of the Scottish People, 1830–1950* (London, 1986), 163.
32   Bruce, *Reminiscences*, 48–9. See also Shewan, *Meminisse Juvat*, 17–18; P C Mitchell, *My Fill of Days* (London, 1937) (hereafter Mitchell, *Fill of Days*), 40, 43–4; L Mackinnon, *Recollections of an Old Lawyer* (Aberdeen, 1935) (hereafter Mackinnon, *Recollections*), 42–3; *Aurora Borealis Academica: Aberdeen University Appreciations, 1860–1889* (Aberdeen, 1899).
33   W S Bruce, ed., *Records of the Arts Class 1864–68. University of Aberdeen* (Aberdeen, 1912), 6.
34   Black and Chrystal, *Robertson Smith*, 31.
35   Ibid., 32–63; Bruce, *Reminiscences*, 17 and following; W R Nicoll, *My Father: an Aberdeenshire Minister, 1812–1891* (London, 1908), 90–6.
36   Recollections of Beveridge in H Cowie, ed., *University of Aberdeen. Record of the Arts Class of 1880–84* (n.p., 1923), 30–1; Mitchell, *Fill of Days*, 35; *AM*, 1 (1883–4), 107–8 and 2 (1884–5), 31; Leask, *Interamna Borealis*, 343; Leask in *AM*, 29 (1911–12), 19.
37   Mitchell, *Fill of Days*, 40.
38   AUL, MS U 291, Literary Society Minutes; R S Walker, 'The Literary Society', *AUR*, 30 (1942–4), 42–51. J M Bulloch analysed the society's choice of authors in *AM*, 6 (1888–9), 75.
39   AUL, MS U 281, Debating Society Minutes, 1860–88; Smith and Cruickshank, *Arts Class 1870–74*, 33–5.
40   *Aberdeen University Gazette*, 5 December 1873, p. 19, and later reports of meetings in *AM*.
41   AUL, MS U 1056, Morice papers (scrapbook with press-cuttings etc, on period 1859–63).
42   P J Anderson, ed., *Rectorial Addresses Delivered in the Universities of Aberdeen, 1835–1900* (Aberdeen, 1902) (hereafter Anderson, *Rectorial Addresses*), 363. This is the best source for rectorials, and includes detailed results as well as accounts of the various incidents. See Appendix II below for a summary of results.
43   M E Grant Duff, *Inaugural Address Delivered to the University of Aberdeen on his Installation as Rector, March 22, 1867* (Edinburgh, 1867) (not reprinted in the Anderson collection).
44   W D Geddes, *Classical Education in the North of Scotland* (Edinburgh, 1869). For the reform question generally, see Anderson, *Education and Opportunity*, 89–91.
45   C Bibby, 'T H Huxley and the universities of Scotland', *AUR*, 37 (1957–8), 140–7.
46   K E Trail, *Reminiscences of Old Aberdeen* (2nd edn, Aberdeen, 1937), 28.
47   *Royal Commission on the Universities of Scotland. Evidence, Part I* (PP, 1878, XXXIII), 339.
48   C A McLaren, 'The Process of curricular change: the pathology question at Aberdeen, 1875–1884', *AUR*, 51 (1985–6), 474–84; A Bain, *Autobiography* (London, 1904), 370–2.
49   Smith and Cruickshank, *Arts Class 1870–74*, 25.
50   *Aberdeen Medical Student*, 22 November 1872, p. 23 (citing *Aberdeen Herald*).
51   Mitchell, *Fill of Days*, 32.
52   Smith and Cruickshank, *Arts Class 1870–74*, 55.
53   Black and Chrystal, *Robertson Smith*, 48.
54   Smith and Cruickshank, *Arts Class 1870–74*, 32. See also K E Trail, *Reminiscences of Old Aberdeen* (2nd edn, Aberdeen, 1937), 109–11.

CHAPTER 2, pp. 32 to 55

1   *University of Aberdeen. Minutes of the General Council*, vol. 1 (Aberdeen, 1898), 57–8, 61–3; *Royal Commission on the Universities of Scotland. Evidence, Part I* (PP, 1878, XXXIII), 148, 811–12.

2   Anderson, *Education and Opportunity*, 325; *Minutes of the University Court of the University of Aberdeen*, vol. 1 (Aberdeen, 1887), 25 November, 20 December 1876; 9 October 1877; 2 August 1878; 11 April, 10 July 1884. See also Leask in *AUR*, 5 (1917–18), 126.

3   *Academic*, 1 (1877–8), 67–8 (January 1878); *AM*, 1 (1883–4), 90 and 2 (1884–5), 91.

4   *Aberdeen Medical Student*, 6 November 1872, 2; 20 December 1872, 37–8.

5   *Aberdeen University Gazette*, 28 November 1873, 12; 16 January 1874, 55; 30 January 1874, 61–3; 20 March 1874, 104–5.

6   Ibid., 20 March 1874, 103, 106–7.

7   *Academic*, 1 (1877–8), 2.

8   On the history of student journalism, see W K Leask, 'The Story of the university magazine: 1836–1914', *AUR*, 2 (1914–15), 1–20; L Donald, 'Alma Mater: Aberdeen University Magazine 1883–1933–1965', ibid., 44 (1971–2), 255–64.

9   *AM*, 5 (1887–8), 3–4, 13–14. For the early years of the SRC, see *Aberdeen University S.R.C. Jubilee Celebrations: 1884–1885, 1934–1935* (n.p., 1935) [AUL, MS U 1067].

10 AUL, MS U 301/1, SRC Minutes 1890–2, 22 October 1892. (This is the earliest volume of these Minutes to survive.)

11 *AM*, 3 (1885–6), 8; 6 (1888–9), 49; 8 (1890–1), 118, 121; 10 (1892–3), 96.

12 Anderson, *Rectorial Addresses*, 384.

13 Ibid., 387.

14 AUL, MS 2798/1/2/3, Bulloch diaries, 6 March 1891; AUL, MS U 301/1, SRC Minutes, 7, 21 March 1891.

15 *AM*, 9 (1891–2), 61; AUL, MS U 301/1, SRC Minutes, 2, 16 May, 13 June, 28 November, 5 December 1891; 6 February 1892.

16 For typical accounts (of the 1896 battle) see Anderson, *Rectorial Addresses*, 389–91 and A F Murison, *Memories of 88 Years, 1847–1934* (Aberdeen, 1935), 219–27. For the detailed arrangements made by committees, see AUL, MS U 346, Minute Book of Huntly committee, 1893.

17 *AM*, 11 (1893–4), 66.

18 Press-cutting of 1893 in AUL, MS 2798/2/3/13, Bulloch scrapbooks.

19 *AM*, 8 (1890–1), 161; J M Bulloch, *The Lord Rectors of the Universities of Aberdeen* (Aberdeen, 1890). See also J M Bulloch, 'The Marquis of Huntly's record rectorship', *AUR*, 24 (1936–7), 196–204.

20 *AM*, 11 (1893–4), 185; 15 (1897–8), 21; 16 (1898–9), 25. The affair is abundantly documented in AUL, MS U 388 and in bound volumes of press-cuttings etc, in AUL; but it is minimised in official histories like W D Simpson, ed., *The Fusion of 1860: a Record of the Centenary Celebrations and a History of the United University of Aberdeen, 1860–1960* (Edinburgh, 1963), 234.

21 *AM*, 18 (1900–1), 146–8, 155, 156–8; AUL, MS U 301/2, SRC Minutes, 16, 20, 23 February 1901.

22 AUL, MS U 307, Rules etc of Aberdeen University Shinty Club.

23 See R D Anderson, 'Secondary schools and Scottish society in the nineteenth

century', *Past and Present*, 109 (1985), 196–201, and 'Sport in the Scottish universities, 1860–1939', *International Journal of the History of Sport*, 4 (1987), 177–88.

24 Mackinnon, *Recollections*, 46.

25 *AM*, 5 (1887–8), 14.

26 D A C Miller, *Aberdeenshire Cricket Association, 1884–1984* (n.p., n.d.), 4.

27 A Shewan, *Spirat Adhuc Amor: the Record of the Gym* (*Chanonry House School*), *Old Aberdeen* (Aberdeen, 1923), 265–75.

28 *AM*, 1 (1883–4), 167–8; 2 (1884–5), 162; 3 (1885–6), 104, 188; 7 (1889–90), 20.

29 *Aberdeen Medical Student*, 6 November 1872, 11; *AM*, 4 (1886–7), 10; W M Ramsay, 'Football & cricket at the university twenty years ago', *AM*, 6 (1888–9), 167–8; AUL, MS U 353, Memoranda of the Aberdeen University Arts Football Club. See also *Aberdeen University Rugby Football Club, 1870–1970* (Aberdeen, n.d.) and A J M Edwards, 'University Rugby Football Club: the early days', *AUR*, 44 (1971–2), 62–7.

30 *AM*, 4 (1886–7), 159.

31 W S Matheson, 'University sports in earlier days', *AUR*, 24 (1936–7), 248–9.

32 Leask in *AM*, 17 (1899–1900), 93.

33 Mackinnon, *Recollections*, 46–7; Mitchell, *Fill of Days*, 34; *AM*, 1 (1883–4), 245 and 2 (1884–5), 140–1.

34 AUL, MS 2798/1/2/3, Bulloch diaries, 19 June 1891.

35 *Aberdeen Medical Student*, 28 February 1873, 107 and 29 March 1873, 130.

36 AUL, MS U 281, Debating Society Minutes, 9 November 1883; *AM*, 1 (1883–4), 12–13; 3 (1885–6), 70, 73.

37 *AM*, 5 (1887–8), 121–2; 6 (1888–9), 42–3; 7 (1889–90), 58–9. See also R B Strathdee, 'The Playing fields of King's', *AUR*, 40 (1963–4), 344–51.

38 *AM*, 10 (1892–3), 15.

39 *AM*, 7 (1889–90), 210.

40 Ibid., 150–1, 180, 187, 200.

41 *AM*, 11 (1893–4), 212, 219.

42 *AM*, 7 (1889–90), 51, 66, 201.

43 *AM*, 8 (1890–1), 151; 12 (1894–5), 25.

44 *AM*, 5 (1887–8), 55.

45 *AM*, 6 (1888–9), 99; 7 (1889–90), 10, 49. See also R B Strathdee, *Aberdeen University Contingent: Officers' Training Corps, Senior Training Corps* (Aberdeen, 1947); *James William Helenus Trail: a Memorial Volume* (Aberdeen, 1923), 28.

46 *AM*, 9 (1891–2), 24.

47 *AM*, 8 (1890–1), 102 (article by Bulloch); 9 (1891–2), 51 (editorial, probably by Bulloch). See also Bulloch in *AUR*, 24 (1936–7), 116–22.

48 Leask, *Interamna Borealis*, 215–17; see also vii–ix, 68–70, 108, 246, and Leask in *AM*, 23 (1905–6), 179–81.

49 See C A McLaren, 'P J Anderson and the history of the university', *AUR*, 51 (1985–6), 83–101.

50 J M Bulloch, *A History of the University of Aberdeen, 1495–1895* (London, 1895).

51 *AM*, 1 (1883–4), 123; 3 (1885–6), 81; 6 (1888–9), 78, 105, 114; 7 (1889–90), 94.

52 J S Blackie, *Musa Burschicosa: a Book of Songs for Students and University Men* (Edinburgh, 1869) and *War Songs of the Germans* (Edinburgh, 1870).

53 *AM*, 6 (1888–9), 71. See also comment in *AM*, 9 (1891–2), 5, and J M Bulloch, 'The Meaning of the "Scottish Students' Song Book" ', *AUR*, 24 (1936–7), 116–22.

54 AUL, MS U 301/1, SRC Minutes, 21 May, 4 June 1892.

55 Bulloch's dramatic interests feature in his diaries in AUL, MS 2798/1/2.

56 AUL, MS U 282, Debating Society Minutes.

57 *AM*, 2 (1884–5), 19, 31.

58 *Academic*, 1 (1877–8), 2–3; *AM*, 17 (1899–1900), 93.

59 *AM Quatercentenary No.*, 16; Temperance Society membership card in AUL, MS U 632, Bulloch scrapbooks.

60 *AM*, 10 (1892–3), 96.

61 E J Bristow, *Vice and Vigilance: Purity Movements in Britain since 1700* (Dublin, 1977), 103–4.

62 *AM*, 1 (1883–4), 151, 170, 191, 224–8; 2 (1884–5), 73, 129–30, 164; 3 (1885–6), 101.

63 *AM*, 6 (1888–9), 95.

64 See, for example, J R Gillis, *Youth and History: Tradition and Change in European Age Relations, 1770–Present* (New York, 1974), 95 and following.

65 *AM Quatercentenary No.*, 16.

CHAPTER 3, pp. 56 to 82

1 *AM*, 8 (1890–1), 1 (probably by Bulloch).

2 *Report of the Committee of Council on Education in Scotland; with Appendix, 1904–1905* (PP, 1905, XXIX), 770. For the teacher training question in general, see Anderson, *Education and Opportunity*, 253–4.

3 M Cruickshank, *A History of the Training of Teachers in Scotland* (London, 1970), 136 and following. For life in the new centre, see A F B Roberts, 'Student life and work, 1910', *Education in the North*, 6 (1969), 12–16, and for students' social backgrounds, J Scotland, 'The Scottish dominie', *Philosophical Journal*, 7 (1970), 131.

4 T Watt and J M Robertson, eds, *University of Aberdeen. Bajans' Jubilee: Record of the Arts Class, 1901–1905* (4th edn, Aberdeen, 1951) (hereafter Watt and Robertson, *Bajans' Jubilee*), 93; T Watt, *Roll of the Graduates of the University of Aberdeen, 1901–1925* (Aberdeen, 1935), 943. On this subject, see also G Mercer and D J C Forsyth, 'Some aspects of recruitment to school teaching among university graduates in Scotland, 1860–1955', *British Journal of Educational Studies*, 23 (1975), 58–77.

5 Watt and Robertson, *Bajans' Jubilee*, 3.

6 R N Gilchrist, ed., *After Graduation: What?* (Aberdeen, 1911).

7 *AM*, 30 (1912–13), 250–1; J Harlaw, *Sandy Gordon Missionar: a Story of Struggle* (London, n.d. [*c.* 1907]), 111–13.

8 *AUR*, 30 (1942–4), 333–4.

9 L Moore, 'The Aberdeen Ladies' Educational Association, 1877–1883', *Northern Scotland*, 3 (1977–80), 123–57. See also L Moore, 'Aberdeen and the higher education of women, 1868–1877', *AUR*, 48 (1979–80), 280–303.

10 N Shepherd, 'Women in the university. Fifty years: 1892–1942', *AUR*, 29 (1941–2), 171–81.

11 For example, *AM*, 24 (1906–7), 152; 26 (1908–9), 223–5; 27 (1909–10), 6.

12 *AM*, 15 (1897–8), 173, 199–200; 16 (1898–9), 9; 17 (1899–1900), 36.

13   *Aberdeen Medical Student*, 3 January 1873, 59.

14   *AM*, 5 (1887–8), 47.

15   *AM*, 8 (1890–1), 50.

16   *AM*, 8 (1890–1), 116, 136, 146, 158–9; 9 (1891–2), 45.

17   AUL, MS U 301/4, SRC Minutes, 29 May 1914; *AM*, 31 (1913–14), 250–2, 261, 272.

18   *Proceedings on the Occasion of the Presentation to the University of Aberdeen of the Portrait of Professor John Harrower, December 19, 1914* (n.p., 1915), 33.

19   *AM*, 12 (1894–5), 126.

20   Ibid., 110.

21   *AUR*, 3 (1915–16), 115–19 (G Watt Smith). On professorial entertaining, see also J F Fraser, *Doctor Jimmy: Some Reminiscences* (Aberdeen, 1980), 39.

22   *AM*, 14 (1896–7), 116, 120.

23   *AM*, 25 (1907–8), 31.

24   *AM*, 29 (1911–12), 214.

25   *AM*, 19 (1901–2), 140, 145, 150; AUL, MS U 301/2, SRC Minutes, 21 June 1902.

26   *AM*, 14 (1896–7), 50; 15 (1897–8), 213.

27   *AM*, 28 (1910–11), 13.

28   *AM*, 27 (1909–10), 61; 30 (1912–13), 118, 278–9.

29   *AM*, 9 (1891–2), 82–4.

30   *AM*, 13 (1895–6), 26, 31.

31   *AM*, 16 (1898–9), 57.

32   *AM*, 18 (1900–1), 105–6.

33   *AM*, 10 (1892–3), 5.

34   *AM*, 9 (1891–2), 33; 11 (1893–4), 165, 176; 12 (1894–5), 55, 75, 109, 115; 13 (1895–6), 133. See also AUL, U 301/2, SRC Minutes, 24 February, 18 December 1894; 25 January 1896.

35   C V A MacEchern, *Memories and Musings* (Edinburgh, 1954), 20–1; F W Law, ed., *University of Aberdeen. Arts Class 1908–1912: Class Record* (Aberdeen, 1954), 89.

36   *AM*, 18 (1900–1), 43, 110. On Simpson, see J A Lillie, *Tradition & Environment in a Time of Change* (Aberdeen, 1970), 25.

37   *Report of the Royal Commission on Physical Training (Scotland)* (PP, 1903, XXX), vol. 2, 446.

38   *AM*, 15 (1897–8), 11–12, 25, 78.

39   *AM*, 13 (1895–6), 128, 148.

40   *AM*, 17 (1899–1900), 91, 106.

41   Ibid., 135, 142. According to *AM*, the magazine *Black and White* had questioned Aberdeen students' patriotism, but I have been unable to find this in the magazine.

42   [Aberdeen] *Evening Express*, 21, 22, 23, 31 May, 1 June 1900; *AM*, 17 (1899–1900), 195–201; R Price, *An Imperial War and the British Working Class: Working-Class Attitudes and Reactions to the Boer War, 1899–1902* (London, 1972), 152–3.

43   *AM*, 18 (1900–1), 8; 19 (1901–2), 5.

44   *AM*, 21 (1903–4), 96–7.

45   *AM*, 29 (1911–12), 85–6.

46   Anderson, *Rectorial Addresses*, 392. No other source mentions this, but Anderson was well-informed.

47   *Evening Express*, 28 October, 4 November 1899; *AM*, 17 (1899–1900), 22–

3, 26. Anderson (392) says only that 'the nomination . . . passed off in comparative quietness'.

48 *Evening Express*, 6 November 1899.
49 Ibid., 13 November 1899; Anderson, *Rectorial Addresses*, 392–3.
50 *AM*, 17 (1899–1900), 22.
51 *AM*, 18 (1900–1), 14, 27–8, 38.
52 *AM*, 19 (1901–2), 59.
53 *AM*, 20 (1902–3), 21.
54 *AM*, 21 (1903–4), 37.
55 Ibid., 190; AUL, MS U 301/3, SRC Minutes, 7 May 1904—but see 7 April, 6 May 1905 for re-establishment of harmony. An American visitor in 1901 was shocked by the rowdiness and ribaldry of the graduation: L Hutton, *Literary Landmarks of the Scottish Universities* (New York, 1904), 133–5.
56 AUL, MS U 301/3, SRC Minutes, 18 June 1904.
57 Ibid., 25 November 1905, 12 May 1906; *AM*, 23 (1905–6), 72.
58 *AM*, 26 (1908–9), 132.
59 *AM*, 25 (1907–8), 212–13.
60 AUL, MS U 282, Debating Society Minutes, 23 October 1908.
61 *AM*, 26 (1908–9), 9, 40–3, 50–1. Copies of rectorial magazines, press-cuttings, etc, for this and other elections, are in various bound collections in AUL.
62 *AM*, 26 (1908–9), 42–3.
63 *AM*, 28 (1910–11), 183.
64 *AM*, 27 (1909–10), 139.
65 K D Buckley, *Trade Unionism in Aberdeen, 1878 to 1900* (Edinburgh, 1955), 153.
66 *AM*, 25 (1907–8), 219.
67 R M MacIver, *As a Tale that is Told: the Autobiography of R M MacIver* (Chicago, 1968), 69–70.
68 See *Concordia: the Annual Journal of the Aberdeen University Peace Society* (n.d.), and AUL, MS U 651, Peace Society Minutes, 1912–14.
69 *AM*, 31 (1913–14), 81 and following.

CHAPTER 4, pp. 83 to 115

1   *AM*, 32 (1914–15), 206 (comma inserted for clarity). See also A Rule, *Students under Arms: being the War Adventures of the Aberdeen University Company of the Gordon Highlanders* (Aberdeen, 1934); *AUR*, 22 (1934–5), 128–31 and 46 (1975–6), 32–44.
2   M D Allardyce, *University of Aberdeen. Roll of Service in the Great War, 1914–1919* (Aberdeen, 1921), vii.
3   *AM*, 34 (1916–17), 30–1, 65–6, 97–8, 112; 35 (1917–18), 41.
4   *AM*, 34 (1916–17), 86; 35 (1917–18), 77.
5   *AUR*, 16 (1928–9), 73; 17 (1929–30), 64; 23 (1935–6), 175–6. See also M Cruickshank, *A History of the Training of Teachers in Scotland* (London, 1970), 160, 168, 171–2.
6   J Harrower, 'Then and now', *AUR*, 6 (1918–19), 3–20. See also reply by J Lees, 'The Present arts course and its critics', ibid., 116–28, and similar conservative views of H J C Grierson in J Clarke, ed., *Problems of National Education, by Twelve Scottish Educationists* (London, 1919), 314–26, and K Stewart in *Nineteenth Century*, 101 (1927), 201–7.

7   See debate on causes of the arts decline between R Knight and A S Ferguson in *AUR*, 30 (1942–4), 12–17, 133–43.

8   *AM*, 37 (1919–20), 61–2; M Sanderson, *The Universities and British Industry, 1850–1970* (London, 1972), 273.

9   Figures in University Grants Committee, *Returns from Universities and University Colleges in Receipt of Treasury Grant* (annual).

10   *AUR*, 24 (1936–7), 263–4.

11   *AUR*, 5 (1917–18), 58–60, 123–31, 261–4; 8 (1920–1), 72, 266.

12   *AM*, 35 (1917–18), 90.

13   AUL, MS U 301/8, SRC Minutes, 7, 13 June 1934, and 1934 election report.

14   *Gaudie*, 3, 10 February 1937; *AUR*, 24 (1936–7), 98–9.

15   *AUR*, 28 (1940–1), 222–4.

16   Linklater's student recollections appeared in two versions: *The Man on my Back: an Autobiography* (London, 1941), and *Fanfare for a Tin Hat: a Third Essay in Autobiography* (London, 1970). See also M. Parnell, *Eric Linklater: a Critical Biography* (London, 1984).

17   AUL, MS U 301/5, SRC Minutes, 18 November 1922; Linklater, *Fanfare for a Tin Hat*, 85. But the issue is minimised by Esslemont in *Aberdeen University S.R.C. Jubilee Celebrations: 1884–1885, 1934–1935* (n.p., 1935) [AUL, MS U 1067], 21.

18   *AM*, 40 (1922–3), 4.

19   Ibid., 59.

20   *AM*, 42 (1924–5), 94, 103.

21   *AUR*, 24 (1936–7), 144 and 39 (1961–2), 217; A Hill, ed., *Third Congress of the Universities of the Empire, 1926: Report of Proceedings* (London, 1926), 186.

22   AUL, MS U 301/5, SRC Minutes, 1 December 1923; *AM*, 45 (1927–8), 243 and 46 (1928–9), 62–3.

23   *AM*, 44 (1926–7), Athletic Number, 2–3; 47 (1929–30), Athletic Number, 5.

24   *Gaudie*, 1 May 1935. On sport, see also *AUR*, 25 (1937–8), 97–8, 266 and 28 (1940–1), 59, 220. Membership figures are in AUL, MS U 795, Athletic Association papers.

25   E Linklater, *The Man on My Back: an Autobiography* (London, 1941), 66–7.

26   *AM*, 49 (1931–2), 75.

27   *AM*, 41 (1923–4), 213.

28   *AM*, 44 (1926–7), 8.

29   *AM*, 38 (1920–1), 208–9.

30   *AM*, 37 (1919–20), 79.

31   *AUR*, 18 (1930–1), 261.

32   For the shows and the gala generally, see J R K Pirie, 'Collections and recollections and a review of revues: a thirty year survey of charities weeks', *AUR*, 33 (1949–50), 417–22 and 34 (1951–2), 25–9. There is a remarkably inaccurate account in *Aberdeen University S.R.C. Jubilee Celebrations: 1884–1885, 1934–1935* (n.p., 1935) [AUL, MS U 1067], 23–5.

33   *AM*, 47 (1929–30), 6.

34   *AM*, 38 (1920–1), 133.

35   *AM*, 39 (1921–2), 25.

36   *AM*, 37 (1919–20), 152–3.

37   Annual membership figures are in R B Strathdee, *Aberdeen University Contingent: Officers' Training Corps, Senior Training Corps* (Aberdeen, 1947), 61.

38   *AM*, 42 (1924–5), 104.

39 *AM*, 43 (1925–6), 4–5, 23, 34–5, 67–8, 83–4, 99–100.
40 *AM*, 37 (1919–20), 73–4.
41 L Kibblewhite and A Rigby, *Aberdeen in the General Strike* (Aberdeen, 1977), 23, 27.
42 *AM*, 43 (1925–6), 316, 340, 342; AUL, MS U 301/5, SRC Minutes, 15 May 1926.
43 *AM*, 47 (1929–30), 77–8, 112, 125, 138; AUL, MS U 301/6, SRC Minutes, 14 December 1929.
44 *AM*, 48 (1930–1), 69–70, 89–90, 96, 105–6, 114–15.
45 Ibid., 87, 103, 116, 139; AUL, MS U 301/6–7, SRC Minutes, 18 February 1928, 29 November 1930.
46 *AM*, 49 (1931–2), 143–4.
47 *AM*, 50 (1932–3), 30.
48 AUL, MS U 283, Debating Society Minutes, 4 November 1927.
49 *AM*, 47 (1929–30), 37.
50 AUL, MS U 283, Debating Society Minutes, 23 January 1931.
51 *AM*, 48 (1930–1), 37; 49 (1931–2), 136; 50 (1932–3), 163.
52 Based on rectorial magazines in bound collections in AUL.
53 AUL, MS 3149, letter from J R K Pirie to J M Bulloch, 9 March 1934, giving inside view of the affair.
54 *AM*, new series, 1 (1933–4), 41–2.
55 Ibid., 59.
56 See, for example, the OTC entry in *Students' Handbook 1934–35*, 119–23.
57 *AM*, new series, 1 (1933–4), 31.
58 AUL, MS U 301/8, SRC Minutes, 2 December 1933, 31 January, 14, 28 February 1934.
59 *AM*, new series, 1 (1933–4), 7, 24; see also 49.
60 Ibid., 87–8.
61 H Grierson, *Essays and Addresses* (London, 1940), 208 (rectorial speech at Edinburgh, 1937).
62 AUL, MS U 301/7, SRC Minutes, 30 May 1931, 27 April 1932.
63 Grieve's message in *Gunpowder: the Magazine of the Students' Party*, 7 November 1933.
64 AUL, MS U 301/8, SRC Minutes, 6 December 1933, 20, 31 January, 14 February 1934.
65 *Gaudie*, 15 October 1935.
66 AUL, MS U 654, Minutes of Intermediary Committee of Court and SRC; *AUR*, 26 (1938–9), 269.
67 See early descriptions in *AM*, 13 (1895–6), 70; 26 (1908–9), 65.
68 *AM*, 49 (1931–2), 35 and 50 (1932–3), 10, 231–2; *Gaudie*, 31 October, 28 November 1934. Downie's cairn was supposed to commemorate a sacrist who had been frightened to death by student horseplay; the story had featured in *Town and Gown*.
69 AUL, MS U 283, Debating Society Minutes, 9 December 1934.
70 AUL, MS U 301/8, SRC Minutes, inserted annual report for 1934–5.
71 *AM*, December 1934, 8–10, 27; March 1935, 10–12, 16–17, 20–1.
72 Ibid., June 1936, 9–10.
73 *Gaudie*, 12 February 1936.
74 L Kibblewhite and A Rigby, *Fascism in Aberdeen: Street Politics in the 1930's* (Aberdeen, 1978).
75 *Gaudie*, 23, 30 November 1937, 18 January 1938.

76 Ibid., 18 January 1938.
77 J Klugmann in J Clark and others, eds, *Culture and Crisis in Britain in the Thirties* (London, 1979), 33. More moderate but essentially similar views are expressed in E Ashby and M Anderson, *The Rise of the Student Estate in Britain* (London, 1970), 61, 85 and B Simon, 'The Student movement in England and Wales during the 1930s', *History of Education*, 16 (1987), 189–203.
78 *Gaudie*, 21 October 1936.
79 AUL, MS U 301/9, SRC Minutes, 3 November 1936.
80 *Gaudie*, 1, 22 May 1935.
81 Ibid., 10, 17 March 1937.
82 Ibid., 18 January 1938.
83 AUL, MS U 301/10–11, SRC Minutes, 22, 24 March 1937; 9, 23 November 1938; 15 February 1939.
84 AUL, MS U 301/11, SRC Minutes, 6, 15 March 1939.
85 Ibid., 7 December 1938; 26 April 1939.
86 *Gaudie*, 13 January 1937.
87 Ibid., 2 December 1936; 13, 20 January, 10 February 1937.
88 Ibid., 25 October, 1 November 1938.
89 Ibid., 22 November 1938; 24, 31 January, 14 March 1939.
90 *Gaudie*, 7 February 1939; see also 3, 10 May 1938.
91 Ibid., 3, 16 May 1939. On Young, see H J Hanham, *Scottish Nationalism* (London, 1969), 166–9.

Appendix I

Figures and Tables

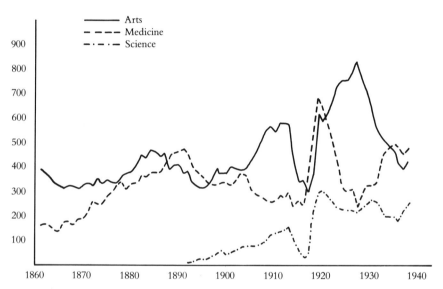

Sources: See Tables 1–3

FIGURE 1   FACULTIES OF ARTS, SCIENCE AND MEDICINE, 1860–
1939

Sources: See Tables 1–3

FIGURE 2   STUDENT NUMBERS, 1860–1939

TABLE 1   STUDENT NUMBERS, 1861–92

	Arts	Divinity	Law	Medicine	Total
1861–2	393	69	12	160	634
1862–3	375	69	8	164	616
1863–4	353	54	12	158	577
1864–5	331	54	8	139	532
1865–6	324	47	15	136	522
1866–7	313	35	20	176	544
1867–8	320	40	12	176	548
1868–9	321	30	10	166	527
1869–70	310	40	15	188	553
1870–1	328	37	12	189	566
1871–2	331	39	19	216	605
1872–3	325	54	21	256	656
1873–4	352	42	13	251	658
1874–5	336	36	14	250	636
1875–6	348	38	25	285	696
1876–7	333	28	21	295	677
1877–8	334	24	13	334	705
1878–9	352	19	19	344	734
1879–80	372	27	23	316	738
1880–1	382	32	23	335	772
1881–2	417	25	35	336	813
1882–3	450	27	23	368	868
1883–4	439	32	28	360	859
1884–5	462	31	30	378	901
1885–6	460	27	27	378	892
1886–7	440	33	18	378	869
1887–8	453	32	27	406	918
1888–9	392	38	29	450	909
1889–90	403	30	24	457	914
1890–1	404	28	24	466	922
1891–2	374	22	46	472	914

NOTE:

These figures were printed annually in the university *Calendar*.

TABLE 2 STUDENT NUMBERS, 1892–1920

	Arts		Science		Divinity	Law		Medicine		Total		Grand Total	Women as % of Total
	M	W	M	W	M	M	W	M	W	M	W		
1892-3	380	—	12	—	19	49	—	452	—	—	—	912	—
1893-4	330	—	13	—	19	45	—	405	—	—	—	812	—
1894-5	299	20	23	—	20	48	—	378	1	768	21	789	2.7
1895-6	278	34	27	—	25	51	—	366	1	747	35	782	4.5
1896-7	282	42	28	—	23	43	—	331	6	707	48	755	6.4
1897-8	286	65	38	—	21	42	—	318	6	705	71	776	9.2
1898-9	307	84	47	—	15	34	—	316	9	715	93	808	11.5
1899-1900	281	95	60	2	16	38	—	325	11	720	108	828	13.0
1900-1	279	98	41	1	11	40	—	316	14	687	113	800	14.1
1901-2	285	117	52	1	14	36	—	308	18	695	136	831	16.4
1902-3	276	120	58	1	15	41	—	333	20	723	141	864	16.3
1903-4	255	131	71	3	14	36	—	354	20	730	154	884	17.4
1904-5	243	147	73	3	14	33	—	355	11	718	161	879	18.3
1905-6	254	168	79	6	22	33	—	308	10	696	184	880	20.9
1906-7	276	190	74	8	21	23	—	292	6	686	204	890	22.9
1907-8	273	235	81	12	21	24	—	277	9	676	256	932	27.5
1908-9	315	239	86	11	20	27	—	266	6	714	256	970	26.4
1909-10	316	253	107	17	18	33	—	255	8	729	278	1007	27.6
1910-11	292	246	114	16	18	20	—	249	14	693	276	969	28.5
1911-12	301	277	121	16	22	15	—	265	18	724	311	1035	30.1
1912-13	304	275	122	25	26	16	—	257	18	725	318	1043	30.5
1913-14	294	275	123	31	25	21	—	269	31	732	337	1069	31.5
1914-15	177	266	79	27	21	12	—	206	39	495	332	827	40.2
1915-16	124	211	40	29	15	3	—	198	64	380	304	684	44.4
1916-17	77	229	21	25	10	2	—	157	91	267	345	612	56.4
1917-18	62	235	20	29	7	4	—	216	124	309	388	697	55.7
1918-19	170	212	154	48	11	9	2	425	156	769	418	1187	35.2
1919-20	331	288	249	51	12	25	4	525	153	1142	496	1638	30.3

NOTES:

1. The figures are from the annual statistical report of the university made under the Universities (Scotland) Act 1889. They were printed as a Parliamentary Paper until 1914, and summarised in the Calendar.

2. Separate figures for women students are not available for 1892-4, and those for 1894-7 may be slightly inaccurate because of ambiguity in the original tables.

3. Students who matriculated only in order to take examinations are included before 1896, but excluded thereafter. They were mostly medical students. Also excluded because they did not matriculate are those who attended special courses for teachers or training-college students.

TABLE 3 STUDENT NUMBERS, 1920–39

	Arts		Science		Divinity		Law		Medicine		Education		Commerce		Total		Grand Total	Women as % of Total	Part-time	
	M	W	M	W	M	W	M	W	M	W	M	W	M	W	M	W			M	W
1920–1	266	315	243	61	10	—	36	4	503	139	3	—	71	4	1132	523	1655	31.6	—	—
1921–2	281	352	213	69	8	—	37	1	462	111	1	—	66	—	1067	533	1600	33.3	—	—
1922–3	290	397	196	70	14	—	22	—	436	89	—	—	50	1	1009	557	1566	35.6	16	—
1923–4	310	432	160	72	14	—	30	3	342	74	—	—	40	1	896	582	1478	39.4	35	—
1924–5	321	434	168	67	15	—	22	1	280	38	—	—	47	1	853	541	1394	38.8	20	—
1925–6	317	439	171	58	19	—	37	—	267	34	—	—	53	4	864	535	1399	38.2	35	—
1926–7	332	451	174	54	19	—	36	1	269	41	2	—	42	4	872	551	1423	38.7	51	3
1927–8	357	479	176	46	24	—	36	2	212	21	3	—	31	7	838	555	1393	39.8	46	3
1928–9	336	428	188	47	20	—	29	3	263	31	2	—	32	5	871	514	1385	37.1	52	8
1929–30	318	396	198	48	14	—	31	2	297	25	1	—	39	4	899	475	1374	34.6	56	10
1930–1	299	347	223	44	24	—	28	1	291	32	1	1	21	2	887	427	1314	32.5	61	10
1931–2	264	306	210	51	29	—	28	4	290	40	1	—	26	3	848	404	1252	32.3	59	14
1932–3	237	297	202	38	24	1	58	6	361	53	1	1	6	3	889	398	1287	30.9	71	7
1933–4	252	254	177	28	36	1	42	6	390	71	2	—	19	6	918	366	1284	28.5	77	11
1934–5	241	246	165	34	26	—	48	5	407	82	1	—	12	6	900	372	1272	29.3	54	11
1935–6	236	226	170	30	39	1	64	—	413	86	3	1	14	4	939	349	1288	27.1	64	9
1936–7	210	203	151	37	36	1	68	2	399	83	3	1	20	1	887	328	1215	27.0	56	10
1937–8	188	211	171	43	42	—	57	3	359	95	5	—	8	2	830	354	1184	29.9	34	5
1938–9	186	239	195	55	35	—	47	6	370	107	5	—	11	2	849	409	1258	32.5	40	7

NOTES:

1. For total figures and part-time students, see University Grants Committee, *Returns from Universities and University Colleges in Receipt of Treasury Grant* (annual). The faculty figures are available only in the version published in the *Calendar*; the *Calendar* does not include them for 1930–1 or from 1936, and for these years the original returns in the University Registry have been used.

2. The totals and faculty sub-totals shown include part-time students, the number of whom is shown in the last two columns. In UGC statistics, the smaller full-time totals were often used.

3. 'Education' refers to students taking the EdB degree.

TABLE 4   BIRTHPLACES OF STUDENTS (%)

	1860s	1908		1924 Arts		1924 All Students	
		Men	Women	Men	Women	Men	Women
Aberdeen city	17.5	28.2	13.6	25.9	21.0	29.6	22.0
Other North East	57.1	50.5	47.5	36.5	49.6	35.0	47.0
Highlands & North	7.6	10.7	27.1	20.0	16.0	15.5	15.2
Other Scottish	8.8	5.8	5.1	8.2	6.7	8.3	7.6
Outside Scotland	8.5	3.9	3.4	9.4	6.7	11.7	8.3
Not known	0.6	1.0	3.4	1.9	—	—	—
No. of cases	343	103	59	85	119	206	132

NOTES:

1. The 1860s column combines information from the following sources: W S Bruce, ed., *Records of the Arts Class 1864–68. University of Aberdeen* (Aberdeen, 1912); A Shewan, ed., *Meminisse Juvat, Being the Autobiography of a Class at King's College in the Sixties* [1866] (Aberdeen, 1905); S Ree, ed., *Records of the Arts Class, 1868–72, University of Aberdeen* (2nd edn., Aberdeen, 1892).

2. The 1908 columns are based on F W Law, ed., *University of Aberdeen. Arts Class 1908–1912: Class Record* (Aberdeen, 1954).

3. The 1924 columns refer to first-year students, and are based on Matriculation Registers: AUL, MS U 8, U 10. 'Arts' covers the arts faculty only, 'all students' also includes science, commerce, law and medicine. Commerce was notable for the high percentage from Aberdeen city (61.9); the highest percentages of non-Scottish students were for women in science (25.0), women in medicine (20.0), and men in medicine (17.5).

4. 'North East' includes Aberdeenshire, Banff, Kincardine, Moray, Nairn. 'Highlands and North' includes Argyll, Bute, Caithness, Inverness, Orkney, Ross and Cromarty, Shetland, Sutherland.

5. For similar information based on matriculation records between 1860 and 1910, and for other Scottish universities, see R D Anderson, *Education and Opportunity in Victorian Scotland: Schools and Universities* (Oxford, 1983), 296–8. Other data on geographical origins are in D I Mackay, *Geographical Mobility and the Brain Drain: a Case Study of Aberdeen University Graduates, 1860–1960* (London, 1969), 68–71, and A C O'Dell and K Walton, 'A Note on the student population of Aberdeen University', *Aberdeen University Review*, 33 (1949–50), 125–7.

TABLE 5   AGES OF ARTS (AND SCIENCE) STUDENTS AT ENTRY

| | Arts Class Records: | | | Matriculation Registers: | | | | | | | | | |
	1860s	1908 M	1908 W	1860	1870	1880	1890	1900 M	1900 W	1910 M	1910 W	1924 M	1924 W
Age													
13	1.2	—	—	—	—	—	—	—	—	—	—	—	—
14	5.0	—	—	5.2	1.1	—	0.9	—	—	—	—	—	—
15	19.8	—	—	28.9	15.3	3.9	1.9	—	—	0.9	1.1	7.0	3.2
16	22.5	1.0	1.7	25.9	19.8	26.8	12.2	3.2	—	2.5	11.6	26.0	17.3
17	16.6	16.5	8.5	19.3	25.2	27.6	29.9	16.8	2.3	11.9	23.2	32.3	50.4
18	8.5	41.8	37.3	5.9	16.2	15.8	25.2	23.2	6.8	41.5	33.7	14.6	15.0
19	7.3	19.4	28.8	5.2	6.3	8.7	17.8	21.1	36.4	18.6	15.8	7.0	7.1
20	5.8	12.6	11.9	3.0	3.6	7.1	4.7	13.7	36.4	9.3	14.7	10.1	6.3
21 and over	12.8	7.8	5.1	5.9	12.6	10.2	7.5	22.1	18.2	15.3	—	—	—
Not known	0.6	1.0	6.8	0.7	—	—	—	—	—	—	—	3.2	0.8
No. of cases	343	103	59	135	111	127	107	95	44	118	95	158	127

NOTES:

1. The table shows the percentage (read vertically) of students falling within each age group at entry.
2. For the 1860s and 1908 sources are as for Table 4. For other years figures are based on matriculation registers. They cover arts students down to 1890, and arts and science students from 1900; for 1924 they also cover commerce.
3. In Anderson, *Education and Opportunity*, 301, figures from the same source are combined with those from other universities to produce Scottish totals. See also J Harrower, *The Age of Entrance to the Arts Curriculum* (Aberdeen, 1912).

TABLE 6   AGES OF STUDENTS AT ENTRY, 1919–39

| | Men: | | | | | Women: | | | | |
	Under 17	17	18	19 and over	No.	Under 17	17	18	19 and over	No.
1919–20	5.5	14.9	23.3	56.4	202	0.8	18.4	43.2	37.6	125
1920–1	3.9	21.0	26.8	48.3	205	3.1	27.3	38.3	31.3	128
1921–2	2.0	25.0	36.8	36.2	152	1.5	19.6	46.4	32.6	138
1922–3	—	10.5	46.3	43.2	190	—	13.6	37.9	48.6	140
1923–4	3.1	26.7	28.6	41.6	161	1.4	17.9	48.3	32.4	145
1924–5	26.0	30.8	21.6	21.6	185	13.4	52.2	22.4	11.9	134
1925–6	16.6	38.1	22.4	22.9	205	9.1	54.6	26.0	10.4	154
1926–7	23.1	36.6	22.0	18.3	186	12.3	49.7	21.9	16.1	155
1927–8	2.2	29.4	35.3	33.2	184	—	23.7	40.2	36.1	169
1928–9	19.8	49.0	15.9	15.3	157	24.8	44.6	27.7	3.0	101
1929–30	20.4	36.0	22.3	21.3	211	17.7	50.4	24.8	7.1	113
1930–1	24.5	38.4	17.9	19.2	151	21.1	51.6	23.4	3.9	128
1931–2	26.4	41.4	17.9	14.3	140	26.1	48.9	20.7	4.4	92
1932–3	6.5	25.6	37.7	30.2	199	3.8	28.3	44.3	23.6	106
1933–4	4.5	27.9	28.5	39.1	179	—	20.7	56.1	23.2	82
1934–5	2.8	28.5	35.2	33.5	179	3.4	39.3	34.8	22.5	89
1935–6	9.6	22.8	38.9	28.7	167	3.7	23.5	45.7	27.2	81
1936–7	4.8	27.4	30.8	37.0	146	5.8	27.9	45.4	20.9	86
1937–8	3.7	36.9	31.0	28.3	187	7.9	37.6	36.6	17.8	101
1938–9	3.2	39.0	31.0	26.7	187	8.5	38.8	34.1	18.6	129

NOTE:

The table covers all full-time graduating students, and shows the percentage (read horizontally) of students falling within each age group at entry. The source is University Grants Committee, *Returns from Universities and University Colleges in Receipt of Treasury Grant* (annual). Despite their official character, the fluctuations in these figures suggest that they may not be entirely trustworthy.

TABLE 7   ARTS STUDENTS, 1860s AND 1908: SOCIAL ORIGINS

| | *1860s* | | *1908* | | | |
| | | | *Men* | | *Women* | |
	No.	%	No.	%	No.	%
Father's occupation						
Landowner	6		—		—	
Minister	39		5		4	
Doctor	19		1		3	
Lawyer	11		1		2	
Teacher	14		11		4	
Other professional	4		4		—	
All professional	93	35.5	22	22.7	13	24.1
Commercial & industrial	38	14.5	9	9.3	6	11.1
Agricultural	76	29.0	12	12.4	14	25.9
Intermediate	29	11.1	20	20.6	8	14.8
Working-class	26	9.9	34	35.1	13	24.1
Not known	81		6		5	
Total	343		103		59	

NOTES:

1. The classification of occupations is that used in Anderson, *Education and Opportunity*, which is itself derived from the report of the Argyll commission on Scottish education in 1868. The commission analysed a sample of 118 Aberdeen students, with results similar to those above: see Anderson, 150–1.
2. Percentages are calculated with reference to the total of known cases.
3. The classification of occupations presents various difficulties. 'Other professional' covers civil servants, army officers, architects, journalists. 'Commercial & industrial' covers the upper business strata: manufacturers, merchants, engineers, managers, bankers, etc. 'Agricultural' includes farmers, crofters (though only 1 parent in the 1860s and 2 in 1908 were specifically so called) and factors, but not labourers. 'Intermediate' includes small businessmen, shopkeepers, clerks, and minor officials. In the 1860s 4 of the 14 'teachers' were professors, but by 1908 this category included more elementary teachers.
4. To avoid ambiguity, it is worth giving a full listing of the Intermediate and Working-class categories.

   1860s, Intermediate: builder/contractor (7), ship's captain/master mariner (6), chemist (2), tailor & clothier (2), bookseller, grocer & weaver, spirit merchant, general merchant, tanner, works overseer, excise officer, inspector of poor (2), inspector of works, road surveyor, railway officer.

   1860s, Working-class: joiner/carpenter (4), saddler & bookbinder, bookbinder, sawmiller, monumental mason, shoemaker (4), woolspinner, blacksmith (2), moulder, postman, army pensioner, farm servant, forester, gardener (2), gamekeeper (2), coachman, labourer.

   1908, Intermediate: builder/contractor (3), shipbuilder, draper (2), warehouseman, tailor/clothier (2), jeweller (2), ironmonger, stationer, shopkeeper, flesher (2), baker (2), grocer, fishcurer, commercial traveller, clerk, cashier, bookkeeper, clerk of works, sanitary inspector (2), stationmaster.

1908, Working-class: joiner/carpenter/cabinet-maker (7), mason (4), shoemaker (3), cooper (2), coachbuilder (2), saddler, tailor's cutter, blacksmith (3), granite polisher, iron turner, tenter, machineman, platelayer, pointsman, road foreman, cleansing foreman, cemetery keeper, watchman, fisherman (4), ferryman, diver, lighthouse-keeper, farm servant (3), shepherd, gardener, estate workman, water bailiff.

5. Fathers' occupations were not recorded consistently in matriculation records until the 1890s. Data for 1900–10 are summarised in Anderson, *Education and Opportunity*, 314–5. These show a lower working-class representation than the 1908 class record (between 14 and 21%), probably because the matriculation records included more 'not known' cases, and because they covered all faculties: arts was the most 'democratic' of the faculties.
6. Some further details of students' social background in 1908–12 are in *Royal Commission on the Civil Service. Appendix to Third Report* (PP, 1913, XVIII), 312 and *Second Appendix to Fourth Report* (PP, 1914, XVI), 561.

TABLE 8   ARTS STUDENTS, 1860s: ORIGINS AND DESTINATIONS

Destinations: Origins:	Church	Medicine	Law	Teaching	Business, Engineering	Army, ICS, etc	Planters and farmers abroad	Miscellaneous	Not known, dead	Total
Landowners	1	1	—	—	—	—	2	—	2	6
Ministers	8	7	4	1	7	5	2	3	2	39
Doctors	1	10	1	—	2	—	4	—	1	19
Lawyers	—	3	4	—	1	—	1	1	1	11
Teachers	4	3	2	4	1	—	—	—	—	14
Other professional	1	1	—	—	—	2	—	—	—	4
Comm. & industrial	6	8	2	3	11	5	2	—	1	38
Agricultural	22	19	—	20	6	3	5	1	—	76
Intermediate	10	7	2	4	1	3	1	1	—	29
Working-class	11	6	—	8	—	—	—	—	1	26
Not known	20	10	4	22	10	2	3	2	8	81
Total	84	75	19	62	39	20	20	8	16	343

NOTES:

1. The table may be read vertically, to show the social origins of students who adopted particular professions, or horizontally, to show the professions adopted by students from particular social origins.
2. Most of those who went into business became 'merchants', bankers, or engineers. 'Army; Indian Civil Service, etc' includes other forms of official service abroad. 'Miscellaneous' includes journalists and literary men and home civil servants. 'Not known, dead' includes those who died at university or shortly after leaving.

TABLE 9   ARTS STUDENTS, 1908: ORIGINS AND DESTINATIONS (MEN)

Destinations:

Origins:	Church	Medicine	Law	Teaching	Business, Engineering	Army, ICS, etc	Planters and farmers abroad	Miscellaneous	Not known, dead	Total
Ministers	1	1	—	1	1	—	—	1	—	5
Doctors	—	—	—	—	—	—	—	1	—	1
Lawyers	—	—	1	—	—	—	—	—	—	1
Teachers	—	2	—	6	1	1	—	1	—	11
Other professional	—	2	—	1	—	1	—	—	—	4
Comm. & industrial	1	1	2	1	2	1	—	1	—	9
Agricultural	5	1	—	4	1	—	—	1	—	12
Intermediate	5	2	—	7	—	—	3	3	—	20
Working-class	8	1	—	20	—	1	—	4	—	34
Not known	1	1	—	2	1	—	—	—	1	6
Total	21	11	3	42	6	4	3	12	1	103

NOTES:

1. The 'miscellaneous' occupations comprise journalists (5), home civil servants (3), scientists (2), a painter, and a farmer in Scotland.
2. Of the 59 women in the class of 1908, all became teachers except seven: one doctor, one civil servant, one librarian, one professional writer, three who did not take up occupations.

TABLE 10 SOCIAL ORIGINS OF STUDENTS, 1924 (Percentages in brackets)

Father's occupation	Arts Men	Arts Women	Commerce Men	Science Men	Science Women	Medicine Men	Medicine Women	Law Men
Minister	5	5	—	—	—	—	—	—
Doctor	1	1	—	2	—	4	2	—
Lawyer	4	1	1	1	—	1	—	1
Teacher	14	5	—	2	—	1	—	—
Other professional	1	—	1	1	—	1	—	1
All professional	25 (29.4)	12 (10.1)	1 (4.8)	6 (11.5)	2 (25.0)	7 (17.5)	2 (40.0)	1 (12.5)
Commercial & industrial	8 (9.4)	20 (16.8)	6 (28.6)	3 (5.8)	1 (12.5)	3 (7.5)	—	3 (37.5)
Agricultural	6 (7.1)	14 (11.8)	1 (4.8)	19 (36.5)	1 (12.5)	7 (17.5)	1 (20.0)	—
Intermediate	18 (21.2)	20 (16.8)	8 (38.1)	10 (19.2)	—	9 (22.5)	2 (40.0)	2 (25.0)
Working-class	17 (20.0)	26 (21.9)	4 (19.1)	6 (11.5)	—	4 (10.0)	—	1 (12.5)
Not known	11 (12.9)	27 (22.7)	1 (4.8)	8 (15.4)	4 (50.0)	10 (25.0)	—	1 (12.5)
Total	85	119	21	52	8	40	5	8

NOTES:

1. Categories as in Table 7. The small numbers involved, and the high proportion of 'not known', make some of the percentages a little artificial.

2. The occupations in the Intermediate and Working-class groups are very similar to those for 1908 in Table 7.

3. Note the high proportion from business families in commerce and law. The large number of farmers' sons in the science faculty reflects the popularity of the BSc in agriculture.

Appendix II

Rectorial Elections

Sir Andrew Leith Hay	240
Edward F Maitland	202

The vote of the nations was equal, and the principal used his casting vote in favour of Maitland.

1863

Lord Russell	231
Mountstuart Grant Duff	133

1866

Mountstuart Grant Duff	245
George Grote	197

1869

Mountstuart Grant Duff	224
Sir William Stirling Maxwell	212

The vote of the nations was equal, and the chancellor (the Duke of Richmond) used his casting vote in favour of Maxwell. Maxwell declined to serve, and a fresh election was held in 1870. It was intended that Grant Duff should be unopposed, but Bernhard Samuelson was put forward in two nations, and 9 votes were recorded for him.

1872

T H Huxley	274
Lord Huntly	220

1875

W E Forster	378
Lord Lindsay	145

1878

Lord Rosebery	302
R A Cross	299

1881

Alexander Bain	444
Sir James Paget	239

1884

Alexander Bain	427
Lord Randolph Churchill	312

1887

G J Goschen	455
John Morley	314

1890

Lord Huntly	430
James Bryce	352

1893

Lord Huntly	348
W A Hunter	252

1896

Lord Huntly	315
A F Murison	300

1899

Lord Strathcona and Mount Royal	unopposed

1902

C T Ritchie	360
H H Asquith	332

1905

Sir Frederick Treves	390
C T Ritchie	153

1908

H H Asquith	435
Sir Edward Carson	370

1911

Andrew Carnegie	unopposed

1914

Winston Churchill	unopposed

1918

Lord Cowdray	unopposed

1921

Sir Robert Horne	557
Sir Donald Maclean	400
Frederick Soddy	253

1924

Lord Cecil of Chelwood	449
Lord Meston	240
C P Trevelyan	101

1927

Lord Birkenhead	316
Sir Archibald Sinclair	307
John Masefield	200

1930

Sir Arthur Keith	312
John Buchan	231

Keith's vote is given as 310 in published sources, but 312 in the official record, AUL, MS M 104.

1933

Walter Elliot	307
G K Chesterton	220
C M Grieve	158
Aldous Huxley	117

1936

It seems impossible to establish exact voting figures for this election. But the candidates in order of success were:

Sir Edward Evans
Sir Josiah Stamp
Sir Alexander Roger
Eric Linklater
Alfred Duff Cooper

1939

Sir Edward Evans	351
Sir Edmund Ironside	268
Sybil Thorndike	159
Lady Douglas Hamilton	42

NOTE ON SOURCES:

Down to 1899, the source is P J Anderson, ed., *Rectorial Addresses Delivered in the Universities of Aberdeen, 1835–1900* (Aberdeen, 1902), and after that date various press sources are used. The official register is AUL, MS M 104, but this book was carelessly kept, and figures were often recorded only for the procurators of the nations, without identifying the candidates.

Bibliographical Note

Detailed bibliographical references have been given in the footnotes, and it seemed unnecessary to list the works consulted separately. Printed sources which appeared before 1906 are listed in a bibliography by P J Anderson in P J Anderson, ed., *Studies in the History and Development of the University of Aberdeen* (Aberdeen, 1906) (also published separately). It may be useful, however, to distinguish the different categories of sources.

1.
General histories of the university. These usually have little on student life.

2.
Official records of university bodies: minutes of the Court, Senatus, and General Council. These have only been used selectively.

3.
Official records of student bodies: minutes of the SRC and of student clubs and societies. These are a major source. Also available in Aberdeen University Library are various collections of press–cuttings, ephemera, programmes, visual material etc, relating particularly to rectorial elections, celebratory occasions, and theatre shows. There are also relevant collections of private papers, notably those of Bulloch.

4.
The student press, chiefly *Alma Mater* and *Gaudie*, and the *Aberdeen University Review*. The more important historical articles in the *AUR* have been cited by title.

5.
Arts class records. Only those actually cited are mentioned in the footnotes. Their publishing history is complex, but they are listed in Anderson's 1906 bibliography and in J M Bulloch, *Class Records in Aberdeen & in America* (Aberdeen, 1916). Other sources of this kind are the manuscript matriculation registers, and the published *Rolls of Graduates*.

6.
Published reminiscences by former students. These may be found in the arts class records, in *AUR*, and in independent publications cited in the footnotes.

7.
Oral and manuscript reminiscences. These are currently being collected as part of the Quincentenary History Project.

Index

Aberdeen, John Campbell Hamilton-Gordon, 7th Earl of Aberdeen 45, 53

Aberdeen Chamber of Commerce 87

Aberdeen Medical Student 34

Aberdeen University Club 5

Aberdeen University Gazette 34

Aberdeen University Review 5

The Academic 34, 52

Academic dress 13, 17, 47–8, 68, 79, 89, 108, 114

Alake of Abeokuta 79

Alma Mater 2 (Pl.1), 8 (Pl.3), 18, 32, 35 (Pl.6), 40, 43 (Pl.9), 45–6, 47, 53, 57, 57 (Pl.11), 62 (Pl.12), 65, 69 (Pl.14), 71, 77, 78, 83, 84, 90 (Pl.18), 91, 93, 98, 102, 104–7, 109 (Pl.22), 110–11, 117

  foundation and early years 34–6

  run by a clique 60

  reorganisation in 1933–4 104–6

  supports pacifism 105–6, 108

  supports Volunteering and the OTC 73, 82, 83–4, 102, 105, 110

  against a hall of residence 88

  critical of university chapel 52, 100

  hostile to women students 63, 66, 79

  theatre and cinema reviews 49, 68, 85, 94, 103–4

Athletic Alma 41 (Pl.8), 74 (Pl.16), 92

Gala Rag 96, 97 (Pl.20), 105

Anatomical and Anthropological Society Proceedings 60

Anderson, Isobel Margaret (MA, 1938) 106 (Pl.21)

Anderson, Peter John (MA, 1872; Librarian, 1894–1926) 47, 79, 88

Angell, Norman 81–2

Arts Class Record 5, 6, 9, 21 (Pl.4), 59, 66–7 (Pl.13)

Askey, Arthur (Rectorial candidate, 1939) 112

Asquith, Henry Herbert, 1st Earl of Oxford and Asquith (Rectorial candidate, 1902; Rector, 1908–11) 78, 80, 143

Bain, Alexander (MA (MC) 1840; Professor of Logic, 1860–80; Rector, 1881–7) 23, 24, 27, 28, 29 (Pl.5), 36, 37, 78, 143

Bain, Lawrence Weir (MB, ChB, 1913) 41 (Pl.8)

Barr, Margaret Miller (MA, 1938) 106 (Pl.21)

Barron, John Hall (MA, 1892) 2 (Pl.1)

Begg, Donald Leslie Bartlett (MA, 1938) 114

Bell, Robert Fitzroy 36

Benson, Percy Hugh (MB, CM, 1873) 43 (Pl.9)

Beveridge, (Alexander Thomas) Gordon (MA, 1889; MB, CM, 1887) 24, 75

Blackie, John Stuart (student (MC), 1821–4 and 1826–9; Professor of Humanity (MC), 1839–52) 48

British Association for the Advancement of Science 98

Brocks, Arthur William (MA, 1948; Director of Physical Education, 1926–58) 91, 92, 100

Brockway, Fenner 110

Bruce, William Straton (MA, 1868; DD, 1897) 23–4

Bryce, James, 1st Viscount Bryce (Rectorial candidate, 1890) 143

Buchan, John, 1st Baron Tweedsmuir (Rectorial candidate, 1930) 103, 144

Bulloch, John Malcolm (MA, 1888) 2 (Pl.1), 5, 17, 35, 38, 40, 44, 47, 48, 49, 53, 55, 116

Bulloch, William (MB, CM, 1890; MD, 1894) 2 (Pl.1)

Bursaries 8–9, 18, 24, 58

Butchart, Henry Jackson (BL, 1905; Secretary to the University, 1920–50) 100, 102

Cairns, David Smith (DD, 1909; LLD, 1938; Principal of Christ's College, Aberdeen) 81, 114

Campbell, Peter Colin (Professor of Greek, 1854; Principal of KC, 1855–60; Principal of the University, 1860–76) 26, 32

Campbell, Eileen M (Asst Director of Physical Education, 1927–38; Adviser to Women Students, 1938–46) 91

Campbell, Margaret Frances (Peggy) (MA, 1939) 106 (Pl.21)

Carnegie, Andrew (Rector, 1911–14) 80, 81, 144

Carnegie Endowment 57, 59

Carson, Edward Henry, 1st Baron Carson (Rectorial candidate, 1908) 80, 143

Cassie, Alexander (MA, 1937) 106 (Pl.21)

Cecil, Edgar Algernon Robert Gascoyne, Viscount Cecil of Chelwood (Rector, 1924–7) 100, 144

Chambers-Hunter, W 111

Champion, Henry Hyde 81

Chancellor 26

Chesterton, Gilbert Keith (Rectorial candidate, 1933) 104, 144

Churches 15, 24, 81, 87
  University Chapel 3, 30, 52, 113

Churchill, Lord Randolph (Rectorial candidate, 1884) 28–9, 29 (Pl.5), 37, 143

Churchill, Sir Winston Leonard Spenser (Rector, 1914–18) 84, 144

Cinemas and films 68, 85, 94, 103–4, 106

College Chimes 34

Concordia 82

Cooper, Alfred Duff, 1st Viscount Norwich (Rectorial candidate, 1936) 111–12, 144

Court (University's governing body) 26, 27, 28, 36, 40, 71, 108

Cowan, Walter (student, 1864–6) 12

Cowdray, Weetman Dickinson Pearson, 1st Viscount Cowdray (Rector, 1918–21) 99, 144

Cramb, Finlay Ross (MA, 1912) 41 (Pl.8)

Cran, Douglas (MB, ChB, 1915) 69 (Pl.14)

Cronwright, Samuel Cron (pen name, Cronwright-Schreiner, S C) 75

Cross, Richard Assheton, 1st Viscount Cross (Rectorial candidate, 1878) 143

Cruden, George (MA, 1873) 43 (Pl.9), 44, 72–3, 91

Curriculum 12–16, 27, 28, 56–7, 69, 71, 86–7, 107–8
  see also Faculties; Subjects studied

Dacre, Arthur *see* James, Arthur Culver

Darwin, Charles and Darwinism 23, 24, 27, 52

Davidson, C 69 (Pl.14)

Dick Bequest 7

Drama   22, 46, 49, 67–8, 104, 117
  Merchant of Venice (1867) 22, *Catch a Weasel* and *Ici on parle français* (1877) 22, *The Area Belle* and *Box and Cox* (1885) 22, *The Chair* (1889) 49, *The Prof* (1890) 49, *The Sweet Girl Undergrad* (1894) 52, *The First Mrs Cranker-Rae* (1895) 52, 74, *Chiselling* (1911) 69 (Pl.14), *A Midsummer Night's Dream* (1918) 85, *She Stoops to Conquer* (1918) 95, *Antigone* (1919) 95 (and Pl.19), *The House of Atreus* (1920) 95, *Oedipus Tyrannus* (1922) 95, *Dangerous Corner* (1937) 95, *Stella the Bajanella* (1922) 96, *Rosemount Nights* (1923) 96, *The Prince Appears* (1924) 96, *One Exciting Evening* (1925) 96, *The Witching Hour* (1926) 96, 98, *Northern Lights* (1927–31) 98, *Aurora Borealis* (1932) 98, *Town and Gown* (1933–4) 98, 106, *The Spice of Life* (1934) 98, *Caravanella* (1935) 98, *Out for the Count* (1936) 98, *That's What You Think* (1937) 98, *Beating Time* (1938) 98, *The Varsity Spirit* (1939) 98
  see also Cinemas; Theatre H M
Duncan, George (MA, 1888)   2 (Pl.1)
Duncan, Capt. William O   73, 75, 76
Duthie, Eric Edmonston (MA, 1926) 101

Education Act, 1918   86
Elliot, Walter (Rector, 1933–6)   104, 108, 144
Empire Universities Congress   91
Emslie, Douglas (student, 1933–6) 103, 110
English influences   13, 32–3, 42, 43, 44, 45, 59, 71, 72
Esslemont, Mary (BSc, 1914; MA, 1915; MB, ChB, 1923; LLD, 1934)   89

Esslemont, Peter   38
Evans, Edward Ratcliffe Garth Russell, 1st Baron Mountevans (Rector, 1936–42)   112, 113, 144–5
Examinations   28, 57, 59

Faculties and their students
  Arts   6, 12, 43, 56, 58, 61, 71, 80, 84, 86, 108, 116, 131 (Fig.2), 132 (Tab.1), 133 (Tab.2), 134 (Tab.3), 135 (Tab.4), 136 (Tab. 5), 138 (Tab.7), 139 (Tab.8), 140 (Tab.9), 141 (Tab.10)
  Commerce   87, 134 (Tab.3)
  Education   134 (Tab.3)
  Divinity   12, 15, 84, 132 (Tab.1), 133 (Tab.2), 134 (Tab.3)
  Law   15–16, 57, 84, 132 (Tab.1), 133 (Tab.2), 134 (Tab.3), 141 (Tab.10)
  Medicine   6, 11, 12, 15, 20, 28, 36, 42, 43, 44, 46, 57, 60, 61, 63, 70, 78, 80, 84, 86, 87, 88, 91, 108, 131 (Fig.2), 132 (Tab.1), 133 (Tab.2), 134 (Tab.3), 141 (Tab. 10)
  Science   56, 58, 86, 131 (Fig.2), 133 (Tab.2), 134 (Tab.3), 141 (Tab. 10)
  Engineering   86
  see also Curriculum; Students; Subjects studied
Fees   18, 71
Fergusson, William Balfour (MB, CM, 1879; MD, 1886)   43 (Pl.9)
Fiddes, John (Jack) (MB, ChB, 1938) 106 (Pl.21)
Forrester, Robert Blair (Lecturer in Political Economy, 1913–22)   81
Forster, William Edward (Rector, 1875–8)   28, 142
From Ploughshare to Pulpit: a Tale of the Battle of Life   3, 4 (Pl.2)
Fyfe, John (Substitute Professor, 1854–60; Professor of Moral Philosophy, 1876–94; University Librarian, 1857–76)   23

Fyfe, Sir William Hamilton (Principal, 1936–48) 113

Galloway, Rudolf William (MB, ChB, 1914) 69 (Pl.14)
Gaudeamus igitur 48, 49, 51 (Pl.10), 94
Gaudie 2, 106 (Pl.21), 110–11, 112–13
Geddes, Sir William Duguid (Professor of Greek, 1855–85; Principal, 1885–1900) 23, 27, 38, 48, 64
General Council 27, 28, 32, 36, 88
General Strike, 1926 99, 101
Giles, Howard 39 (Pl.7)
Gillies, Kenneth (MA, 1891; MB, CM, 1895) 2 (Pl.1)
Gordon, George Alexander Connell (MB, ChB, 1914; DPH, 1920) 41 (Pl.8)
Goschen, George Joachim, 1st Viscount Goschen (Rector, 1887–90) 37–8, 40, 49, 143
Graduation ceremonies 30, 70, 78
Graham, Robert Bontine Cunninghame 103
Grant, William Presslie (student, 1888–90) 2 (Pl.1)
Grant Duff, Sir Mountstuart Elphinstone (Rectorial candidate, 1863; Rector, 1866–72) 27, 30, 142
Gray, Malcolm (MA, 1939) 106 (Pl.21)
Gray, Robert Aikman (MB, CM, 1874; MD, 1879) 43 (Pl.9)
Greenhorne, Marcus Fernando Hillarion (BSc(Eng.), 1931) 109 (Pl.22)
Grey, Edward, 1st Viscount Grey of Falloden (Rectorial candidate, 1899) 77
Grierson, Sir Herbert John Clifford (MA, 1887; Professor of English, 1894–1915) 36, 47, 69, 107
Grieve, Christopher Murray (pseudonym Hugh MacDiarmid) (Rectorial candidate, 1933) 104, 108, 144

Gripper, Walter (MA, 1875) 43 (Pl.9)
Grote, George (Rectorial candidate, 1866) 142
Gunn, Neil Miller 103

Haldane, Richard Burton, 1st Viscount Haldane of Cloan 76
Hall, John George (MB, CM, 1873; MD, 1882) 43 (Pl.9)
Halls of residence 32–3, 34, 63, 87–8, 118
  proposal for an 'Elphinstone Hall' 88
Hamilton, Lady Douglas (Rectorial candidate, 1939) 145
Harrower, John (MA, 1876; Professor of Greek, 1886–1931) 21 (Pl.4), 64, 71, 86, 95 (and Pl.19)
Hay, Sir Andrew Leith (Rectorial candidate, 1860) 26, 142
Hay, Matthew (LLD, 1927; Professor of Forensic Medicine, 1883–1926) 71
Hein, Gustav (Lecturer in German, 1898–1903) 75
Hendry, Neil Geddes Clarkson (MB, ChB, 1939) 106 (Pl.21)
Henry, Robert (MA, 1929) 102
Honours degrees 14, 56, 60
  see also Curriculum
Horne, Robert Stevenson, 1st Viscount Horne of Slamannan (Rector, 1921–4) 100, 144
Hospitals
  The Dispensary 15, 75
  Royal Infirmary 7, 94, 96
  Royal Lunatic Asylum 15, 42
  Sick Children's 15
Hunt, William George Philip (MA, 1912) 74 (Pl.16)
Hunter, William Alexander (MA, 1864; LLD, 1882; Rectorial candidate, 1893) 143
Huntly, Charles Gordon, 11th Marquess of Huntly (Rectorial candidate, 1872; Rector, 1893–9) 40, 46, 68, 70, 76, 142, 143

Huxley, Aldous Leonard (Rectorial candidate, 1933)   104, 144
Huxley, Thomas Henry (Rector, 1872–5)   27–8, 34, 40, 142

Indian Civil Service   11, 12, 33
Inglis, Elsie Maud   85
Innes, John Fraser (MB, CM, 1875; MD, 1894)   43 (Pl.9)
Innes, John William (MA, 1910; MB, ChB, 1915; DPH, 1919)   74 (Pl.16)
Ironside, Sir Edmund (Rectorial candidate, 1939)   145

James, Arthur Culver (stage name, Arthur Dacre) (MB, CM, 1874; MD, 1877)   49
Johnson, Allan (student, 1882–3 and 1891–3)   74–5
Johnston, David (Professor of Biblical Criticism, 1893–9)   40
Johnstone, (George) Erskine (MB, ChB, 1939)   106 (Pl.21)
Jordan, David Starr   82
Joyce, William   110

Keig, the Free Manse, see Smith, William Robertson
Keith, Sir Arthur (MB, CM, 1888; MD, 1894; Rector, 1930–3)   102–3, 144
Kellas, Arthur Roy Handersyde (MA, 1936)   108, 110
Kelman, John   81
Kelsall, Moultrie   98, 106 (Pl.21)
King's College   1, 6, 23–4, 26, 42, 43, 45, 48, 69, 71, 94, 102, 118
Elphinstone Hall   94
see also Churches—University Chapel
Kirton, John (MA, 1911; MB, ChB, 1914; MD, 1921)   74 (Pl.16)

Lang, John Marshall (Principal, 1900–1909)   81

Leask, William Keith (MA, 1877)   3, 22, 34, 44, 47, 49, 52, 66, 79, 88
Leavis, Queenie Dorothy   106
Leith-Ross, (Elizabeth) Jean (student, 1935–7)   106 (Pl.21)
Life at a Northern University   3, 17, 34, 79
Lindsay, James Ludovic, 26th Earl of Crawford (Rectorial candidate, 1875)   142
Linklater, Eric Robert Russell (MA, 1925; LLD, 1946; Rectorial candidate, 1936; Rector, 1945–8)   89, 90 (Pl.18), 93, 96, 98, 99, 100, 103, 111–12, 144
Lowe, Donald Neil (MA, 1912)   41 (Pl.8)

Macaulay, Alexander (student, 1910–12)   41 (Pl.8)
MacCormick, John Macdonald   103
McCulloch, William Edward (MB, ChB, 1923)   99
MacDiarmid, Hugh   see Grieve, Christopher Murray
Macdonald, Alistair Cameron (MA, 1913; MB, ChB, 1916)   74 (Pl.16)
MacDonald, George (MA (KC), 1845; LLD, 1868)   3
MacEchern, Christian Victor Aeneas (MA, 1907)   72
MacGillivray, George Mortimer (MB, ChB, 1912)   74 (Pl.16)
McHardy, William Duff (MA, 1912; BD, 1935; DD, 1958)   103
M'Intosh, Lilian (MA, 1937)   106 (Pl.21)
MacIver, Colin Crichton (MA, 1936)   107, 108, 112
MacIver, Norman Crichton (MA, 1939)   112, 113, 114
MacIver, Robert Morrison (Lecturer in Political Science and Sociology 1907–16)   81
Mackay, Adam (student, 1882–91)   2 (Pl.1)

Mackenzie, Angus Muriel (Mure) (MA, 1912; MA (Hons), 1913; DLitt, 1924) 63

Mackenzie, Sir (Edward Montague) Compton 103

Mackenzie, Donald (MA, 1913) 41 (Pl.8)

Mackenzie, John Moir (MA, 1911; MB, ChB, 1915) 69 (Pl.14)

Mackenzie, Kenneth Pirie (MA, 1910; MB, ChB, 1914) 69 (Pl.14)

Mackenzie, William Andrew (student, 1887–91) 48

McKerron, Robert Gordon (MA, 1884; MB, CM, 1888; MD, 1898; Professor of Midwifery, 1912–36) 36, 91

Mackinnon, Capt Lachlan Jnr (MA, 1875) 74 (Pl.16)

Mackintosh, Ashley Watson (MA, 1888; MB, CM, 1893; MD, 1896; Professor of Medicine, 1912–28) 36, 37, 45, 91

McLaggan, James Murray (MB, ChB, 1913) 74 (Pl.16)

McLaren, Moray David Shaw 103

Maclean, Alexander George (MB, ChB, 1913) 41 (Pl.8)

Maclean, Sir Donald (Rectorial candidate, 1921) 100, 144

Maclean, Neil Nathaniel (MA (KC), 1859) *see Life at a Northern University*

Maclennan, Kenneth (BSc (Agric.), 1912) 41 (Pl.8)

MacLeod, George Fielden, Baron MacLeod of Fuinary 113

Macmillan, Donald (MA, 1887) 2 (MA 1922; LLB 1924) (Pl.1)

Macrae, Victor Charles (James) (MA, 1914) 41 (Pl.8)

Maitland, Edward Francis, Lord Barcaple (Rector, 1860–3) 26, 142

Mammen, John Humphrey (student, 1909–12) 69 (Pl.14)

Marischal College 1, 6, 26, 30, 38, 42, 43, 45, 60, 64, 68, 69, 72, 79, 80, 85, 94, 118
Mitchell Hall 70, 78, 92–3, 101, 108

Marr, David Murdoch (MB, ChB, 1914; MD, 1919) 74 (Pl.76)

Martin, William (Professor of Moral Philosophy, 1846–1876) 23

Masefield, John Edward (Rectorial candidate, 1927) 101, 102, 144

Maxton, James 110

Maxwell, Sir William Stirling (Rectorial candidate, 1869) 27, 142

Medical Students' Shaver 33

Meston, James Scorgie, 1st Baron Meston of Agra (Rectorial candidate, 1924) 100, 144

Militarism and pacifism 73–6, 81–2, 99, 100–2, 105, 110, 112, 114
see also Volunteering

Milne, John Irvine Wallace (MA, 1931) 106–7

Minto, William (MA, 1865; Professor of Logic, 1880–93) 25, 29 (Pl.5)

Mitchell, Anthony (MA, 1890) 2 (Pl.1)

Mitchell, Charles (student (MC), 1839–40; LLD, 1893) 70

Mitchell, Peter Chalmers (MA, 1884) 24, 29

Mollison, William Loudon (MA, 1872; LLD, 1897) 8 (Pl.3), 21 (Pl.4)

Morley, John, 1st Viscount Morley of Blackburn (Rectorial candidate, 1887) 37, 143

Morrison, James (MA, 1911; MB, ChB, 1914) 74 (Pl.16)

Mosley, Sir Oswald Ernald 110, 111

Mundie, Miss 71

Munich crisis, 1938 114

Munro, Donald 99

Murison, Alexander Falconer (MA, 1869; LLD, 1893; Rectorial candidate, 1896) 143

Music
Choral Society 25, 48, 50–1 (Pl.10), 68, 93, Music Hour 93, Music Society 93, Singing 20,

Music (*continued*)
   21–2, 48, 68, 75, 93, 94, Smoking 20, 21–2, 48, 68, 75, 93, 94,
   Smoking concerts 48–9, 75, 78,
   80, University jazz bands 93
Music Hall, The   30, 38, 45, 46

Neil, Robert Alexander (MA, 1870;
   LLD, 1891)   7, 8 (Pl.3)
Newcombe, Charles Frederic (MB,
   CM, 1873; MD, 1878)   43 (Pl.9)
Newcombe, Frank (student, 1872–3
   and 1876–7)   43 (Pl.9)
Newspapers   viii, 35, 77, 78, 105
Nicoll, William Robertson (MA, 1870;
   LLD, 1890)   3, 17, 18, 24
North of Scotland College of Agri-
   culture   56–7
Norrie, William   98

Officers' Training Corps (OTC)   *see*
   Volunteering
Ogilvie, Thomas White (MB, CM,
   1892)   2 (Pl.1)
Oral evidence   viii

Pacifism   *see* Militarism and pacifism
Peace Ballot, 1935   112
Pirie, Lewis (student, 1864–6)   12
Pirie, William Robertson (Professor of
   Divinity, MC, 1843–60; Church
   History,   1860–77;   Principal,
   1877–85)   33, 64
Ponsonby, Arthur Augustus William
   Henry, 1st Baron Ponsonby of
   Shulbrede   101
Pratt, James Davidson (MA, 1912; BSc,
   1913)   41 (Pl.8)
Principal   26
Professors   *see* University teachers
Pullin, Frank Bingley (student, 1872–4)
   43 (Pl.9)

Raitt, Douglas Stewart (BSc, 1926;
   PhD, 1930; DSc, 1937)   98
Ramsay, William Mitchell (MA, 1871;
   Professor of Humanity, 1886–

1911)   8 (Pl.3), 40–1, 42, 43, 65,
   71
Rattray, Patrick Whyte (MA, 1881;
   MB, CM, 1885)   36
Recano, John Baptist (student, 1886–7
   and 1888–90)   49
Rector   26, 29 (Pl.5), 39 (Pl.7), 145
   possibility of a student Rector   28
   working and non-political Rectors
      26, 40, 76, 79, 102, 104, 112
Rectorial elections   26, 101, 142–5
   (App. II)
   (1860) 26; (1863, '66, '69, '72) 27;
   (1875, '78, '81, '84, '87) 28, 29
   (Pl.5), 37, 38; (1890) 38, 40,
   (1893) 40; (1896) 39 (Pl.7), 40,
   (1899) 77; (1902) 78; (1905) 79;
   (1908) 80; (1911) 80; (1918) 99;
   (1921)   99–100;   (1924)   100;
   (1927) 101; (1930) 102–3; (1933)
   104, 108; (1936) 112; (1939) 112
Reid, Sir George   48
Reid, Sheila Macdonald (MA, 1939)
   106 (Pl.21)
Rennet, David (LLD, 1885; Mathematics coach, 1856–?)   14, 21
   (Pl.4)
Restaurants, public houses and dance
   halls
   Duffus's 19; The Grand Hotel 21
      (Pl.4); The Grill 67; Jimmy
      Hay's 67; Johnny Macdonald's
      Pie Shop 53; Kennaway's 65,
      66, 83; The Lemon Tree 19, 53;
      The Palais de Danse 94; The
      Pavilion 94; The Red Lion 19;
      Watson's 67; The West End
      Cafe 65; Woolworth's 94
Revues   *see* Drama
Ritchie, Charles Thomson, 1st Baron
   Ritchie of Dundee (Rector, 1902–
   5; Rectorial candidate, 1905)   78–
   9, 143
Robert Gordon's Institute of Tech-
   nology   96
Roberts, Frederick Sleigh, 1st Earl
   Roberts of Kandahar   82

Robson, Robert Boyd (MB, ChB, 1902) 2 (Pl.1)

Roger, Sir Alexander (Rectorial candidate, 1936) 112, 144

Rose, Alexander McGregor (student, 1863–7) 43 (Pl.9)

Rose, John (BSc (Agric.), 1911) 41 (Pl.8)

Rosebery, Archibald Philip Primrose, 5th Earl of Rosebery (Rector, 1878–81) 28, 30, 44, 143

Royal Commission on Physical Training, 1903 72

Royal Commission on the Universities of Scotland, 1876 28

Russell, John, 1st Earl Russell (LLD (MC), 1848; Rector, 1863–6) 27, 142

Sacrists 16

Samuelson, Sir Bernhard, 1st Bt (Rectorial candidate, 1870) 142

Schools 7, 9, 42, 54, 58
Aberdeen Grammar School 9, 60, 72
Chanonry House School ('The Gym') 9, 42, 43
Old Aberdeen Grammar School ('The Barn') 9
Robert Gordon's College 60, 72

Scott, Anne Elizabeth (Betty) (MA, 1938) 106 (Pl.21)

Scottish Education Department 10, 59

Scottish Students' Songbook 48

Senatus 16, 27, 28, 37–8, 48, 64, 75, 78, 100, 104, 108

Shennan, Theodore (LLD, 1937; Professor of Pathology, 1914–36) 91

Shepherd, Anna (Nan) (MA, 1915; LLD, 1964) 84, 103

Sheppard, Hugh Richard Lawrie (Dick) 113

Shewan, Henry Alexander (MA, 1928; LLB, 1932) 102

Simpson, H F Morland 72

Sinclair, Sir Archibald Henry Macdonald, 1st Bt (Rectorial candidate, 1927) 101, 144

Skinner, Alexander Hugh (MA, 1903; MB, ChB, 1907; MD, 1909) 41 (Pl.8)

Skinner, Charles Gordon Lennox (MB, CM, 1873; MD, 1877) 43 (Pl.9)

Smith, Frederick Edwin, 1st Earl of Birkenhead (Rectorial candidate, 1914 and 1927) 84, 101–2, 144

Smith, Sir George Adam (Principal, 1910–36) 76, 81, 82, 84, 100, 102, 113

Smith, George Michie (MA, 1866) 24

Smith, Isabella Jane (MA, 1917) 84

Smith, James Lind (MA, 1911; MB, ChB, 1914; DPH, 1920) 74 (Pl.16)

Smith, Robert (MA, 1873; MB, CM, 1875; MD, 1880) 8 (Pl.3)

Smith, Walter Chalmers (MA (MC), 1841; LLD, 1876) 3

Smith, William Robertson (MA, 1865; LLD, 1882) 24
'The Smith legend' 47; 'Shon Campbell' 48; The Free Manse of Keig 24, 116

Soddy, Frederick (Professor of Chemistry, 1914–19; Rectorial candidate, 1921) 99, 144

Sorrie, George (MA, 1872) 7

Sport 32–3, 34, 41–6, 71–3, 84, 85, 89–92
Athletic Assoc. 45, 46, 72–3, 92
Field Committee 72
gymnasium 44–5, 69–70, 72, 91
inter-university games 44, 89
pavilion 71
playing fields 44–5, 71–2, 84, 85, 92
professionalism in sport 44, 72
swimming pool and squash courts 92
Wednesday afternoons for sport 91
women and sport 73, 91–2

Sport (*continued*)
see also Sporting Clubs, Student societies
Sporting clubs
Athletic 44, 45; Association football 45, 72, 73; Boat 44, 68, 69 (Pl.14), 73, 89; Cricket 41, 42, 45, 73; Cycling 73, 91; Gymnastic 72, 73; Golf 44, 73, 92; Hockey 73, 92; Mountaineering 91; Open Air 91; Rugby football 42–4, 43 (Pl.9), 45, 73, 117; Shinty 41 (Pl.8), 45, 73; Shooting 74 (Pl.16); Squash 92; Swimming 44, 73, 92; Tennis 45, 73, 92
see also Sport, Student societies
Stables, Gordon (MB, CM, 1862) 3, 4 (Pl.2)
Stamp, Josiah Charles, 1st Baron Stamp (Rectorial candidate, 1936) 112, 144
Strachan, (Margaret) Vivien (MA, 1937) 106 (Pl.21)
Strathcona and Mountroyal, Donald Alexander Smith, 1st Baron Strathcona and Mountroyal (Rector, 1899–1902) 77, 143
Struthers, Sir John (Professor of Anatomy, 1863–89) 23, 27, 29 (Pl.5), 53
Student community
absence of corporate life 18–19, 37, 53–4, 87–9
bazaars 44–5, 46, 52, 70, 72, 96
dinners and class suppers 20–1, 21 (Pl.4), 49, 53, 64, 93
esprit de corps 5, 12, 44, 47, 60, 116
galas and charities campaign 96–8, 97 (Pl.20), 101
growth of corporate identity 1, 32–55, 45–47, 49, 100, 116
influence on academic affairs 40–1
journalism 2, 20, 29, 33–6
picnics 64, 66–7 (Pl.13), 91
ragging and rowdyism 16, 20, 23, 26–7, 28–31, 37–41, 46, 54–5,

61, 68, 69–70, 75, 77–80, 89, 93, 101–2, 108, 116, 118
torchlight processions 30, 37–40, 49
vandalism 15
see also Drama, Music, Rector, Rectorial Elections, Sport, Sporting clubs, Student societies, Student Union, Students' Representative Council
Student societies represented on the SRC 36
Agricultural Discussion Soc. 61; Anatomical and Anthropological Soc. 60; Catholic Students' Fellowship 93; Celtic Soc. 20, 25, 76; Choral Soc. 25, 48, 50–1 (Pl.10), 68, 93; Christian Assoc., Fellowship, Union, Student Christian Movement 52, 61, 81–2, 85, 91, 93, 99, 113; Classical Soc. 60; Commerce Soc. 93; Conservative and Unionist Assoc. 37, 78, 80, 99, 111, 114; Debating Soc. 20–1, 25, 35–6, 44, 47, 49, 52, 53, 61, 68, 72, 76–7, 81, 82, 93, 96, 98, 102, 108, 111, 114, 117; Dramatic Soc. 49, 52, 68, 95, 106 (Pl.21); Engineering Club 93; Episcopal Club 93; Ethical Soc. 24, 52, 75; Forestry Club, 93; Free Church Students' Assoc. 20; Geology Club 93; Hellenic Soc. 23; History Club 93; Independent Assoc. 102; International Relations Soc. 112, 114; International Students' Service Branch 112; Juridical Soc. 60; Labour Club 99, 101, 107, 114; League of Nations Union and Soc. 99, 112, 114; Liberal Assoc. and Club 78, 80, 99, 114; Literary Soc. 20, 25, 49, 60, 61, 68, 93; Mathematical Soc. 60; Medical Soc. 20; Missionary Settlement for Uni-

versity Women 81; Missionary Soc. 21; Modern Languages Soc. 61, 85; Musical Soc. 93; Nationalist Assoc. 103; Overseas Club 93; Peace Council 114; Peace Soc. 81–2, 84, 99, 114; Philosophical Club 60; Reform Club 112, 114; Scottish Women's First-Aid Corps University Branch 85; Socialist Club 103, 107, 111; Sociological Soc. 81–2, 85, 99, 114; Temperance Soc. 53; Theological Soc. 61; Toc H University Branch 93; University Working Party and Canteen 85; White Cross Union 53; Woman Suffrage Assoc. 79–80, 99; Women's Debating Soc. 61, 65, 76, 85; Women's Dramatic Soc. 85, 95; Women's Medical Soc. 61; Women's Political Assoc. 99

Student Union 32, 45, 54, 69, 70 (and Pl.15), 77, 85, 94, 117

Women's Union 94

Students
  age 7, 10, 24, 36, 54–5, 56, 59, 87, 136 (Tab.5), 137 (Tab.6)
  backgrounds 1, 7, 10–13, 15, 32–3, 59, 60, 81, 87, 101, 103, 116–18, 135 (Tab.4), 138 (Tab.7), 139 (Tab.8), 140 (Tab.9), 141 (Tab.10)
  bajans, semis, tertians, magistrands, lambs 13, 20, 21, 33, 37, 55, 89, 94, 108, 109 (Pl.22)
  bajanellas and semilinas 61
  careers 11–13, 58–9, 60, 86–7, 103, 105, 111, 116, 139 (Tab.8), 140 (Tab.9)
  cost of living 18, 33, 65, 71, 87–8
  cultural interests 15, 19, 23–5, 49, 57 (Pl.11), 68, 85, 93, 94–5, 103–5, 110, 117
  dancing 63–4, 84, 85, 92–4, 117

drinking 19–20, 49, 52–3, 64, 67, 69–70, 92–3
Highland 3, 7, 8, 11, 20, 25–6, 48, 59
lodgings 3, 4 (Pl.2), 16–18, 37, 57 (Pl.11), 87–8
  see also halls of residence
numbers 1, 6, 83–4, 86, 130 (Fig.1), 131 (Fig.2), 132 (Tab.1), 133 (Tab.2), 134 (Tab.3)
politics 25–6, 28, 30, 37, 78–82, 84–5, 98–105, 107, 108–15
religion 34, 52, 81, 93, 100, 113–14
sex 22–3, 53, 63, 105, 107
social life 19–23, 48–49, 63–71, 92–8, 116–18
travel 15, 36
women 52, 55, 56, 58, 61–7, 62 (Pl.12), 68, 70, 71, 73, 78, 79–80, 84, 86, 89, 92, 94, 117, 130 (Fig.1), 133 (Tab.2), 134 (Tab.3), 135 (Tab.4), 136 (Tab.5), 137 (Tab.6), 138 (Tab.7), 141 (Tab.10)
women's suffrage 79–80
  see also Drama, Faculties, Music, Rector, Rectorial Elections, Sport, Student community, Student Societies, Student Union, Students' Representative Council, Volunteering

Students' Representative Council (SRC) 31, 32, 36–41, 45, 48, 52, 60, 69, 71, 72, 79, 80, 81, 84, 88, 91, 92–3, 101, 102, 106, 107–8, 110, 113, 117
  Amusements C'ttee 49, 64, 68, 85, 94
  charities campaign 96–8, 101
  Inter-Universities Conferences 36, 88, 99
  women 61–3, 84

Subjects studied
  Accountancy 87; Agriculture 56; Banking 87; Business Studies 87; Christian Evidences 14; Commerce 87; Commercial French 87; Economic Geogra-

Subjects studied (*continued*)
> phy 87; Economics 56; English 14, 25, 56; Forestry 56; Geology 23, 86; Greek 7, 13–14, 27, 28, 56, 87; History 27, 56; Latin 7, 9, 13, 56, 87; Law 57; Logic 56, 86; Mathematics 7, 12, 14, 87, 107; Mental Philosophy 14, 86; Mercantile Law 87; Modern Languages 27, 56, 86; Moral Philosophy 14, 86; Natural History 14; Natural Philosophy 14, 87; Pathology 28; Political Science 56; Science 12, 27; Zoology 23, 86
> *see also* Curriculum, Faculties

Sutherland, William Henry (MA, 1914)   82, 84

Swaine, Charles Lethbridge (MB, CM, 1874; MD, 1889)   43 (Pl.9)

Symon, James David (MA, 1892)   2 (Pl.1)

Taylor, Sir Thomas Murray (MA, 1919; LLB, 1922; Professor of Law, 1935–48; Principal, 1948–62)   99

Teacher training and Training College   7, 58, 59, 60, 72, 86, 88, 96

Territorial Army   *see* Volunteering

Terry, Charles Sanford (LLD, 1931; Professor of History, 1903–30) 68

Teunon, Clara Macandrew (MA, 1937)   106 (Pl.21)

Theatre, H M   49, 64, 68, 94, 98, 104
> *see also* Drama

Thorndike, Sybil (Rectorial candidate, 1939)   112, 145

Tighe, Charles (MB, ChB, 1916)   41 (Pl.8)

Topping, Andrew (MA, 1911; MB, ChB, 1914; MD, 1923; DPH, 1923)   74 (Pl.16)

Trail, Samuel (MA (KC), 1825; LLD, 1847; DD, 1852; Professor of Systematic Theology, 1867–87)   27, 29 (Pl.5)

Trevelyan, Sir Charles Philips, 3rd Bt (Rectorial candidate, 1924)   100, 144

Treves, Sir Frederick (Rector, 1905–8)   79, 143

Troup, John (student, 1873–6)   43 (Pl.9)

Tullibardine, John George Stewart-Murray, Marquess of Tullibardine   76

Turner, Stanley Horsfall (Lecturer in Political Economy, 1904–12)   81

University Grants Committee (UGC)   87, 88

University of Edinburgh   1, 22, 26, 36, 49, 53, 61, 101

University of Glasgow   1, 22, 26, 36, 45, 61, 101, 103, 104

University of St Andrews   26, 32, 36, 43, 44, 48

University reform   25, 27, 36, 108

Universities (Scotland) Act (1858)   6, 26; (1889)   36, 56

Universities, Scottish   1, 28, 32, 85, 91, 102

University teachers
> Professors   16, 23, 33, 35, 64–5, 71, 73, 80, 81, 91
> Lecturers   56, 61
> Assistants   16, 47, 61

Vacations   *see* Curriculum

Volunteering   46, 68, 73–6, 81, 83–4, 117
> The Battery   46, 73
> The Bearer Co., Ambulance Corps, Medical Staff Corps, Medical OTC   46, 52, 73, 74, 100
> Officers' Training Corps (OTC)   76, 84, 100, 101, 102, 104, 105, 106, 111, 113, 115
> Scottish Horse Unit   76
> U Company, Gordon Highlanders   73, 74, 74 (Pl.16), 76, 82, 83–4
> *see also* Militarism and Pacifism

Wallace, Gordon Profeit (MA, 1934; MB, ChB, 1939)   106 (Pl.21)

War
  Boer War   72–6, 77, 78
  First World War   83–8, 86, 88–9
  Second World War   114–15
Wardrop, Douglas (MB, CM, 1875) 43 (Pl.9)
Wharry, Robert (MB, CM, 1875; MD, 1878)   43 (Pl.9)

Wilson, George (MA, 1913)   72
Wood, Wendy   103
Wodehouse, Pelham Grenville   107
Workers' Educational Assoc.   81

Yates, William Butler   68
Young, Douglas Cuthbert Colquhoun (Asst in Greek, 1938–41)   114